Justus Roe

Roe's Hotel Guide for Commercial Travellers

Justus Roe

Roe's Hotel Guide for Commercial Travellers

ISBN/EAN: 9783337292584

Printed in Europe, USA, Canada, Australia, Japan

Cover: Foto ©Andreas Hilbeck / pixelio.de

More available books at **www.hansebooks.com**

ROE'S
HOTEL GUIDE,

~ FOR ~

COMMERCIAL TRAVELLERS.

1876.

Containing the Names of Hotels, Names of Proprietors, Rates per Day and parts of Day, per Week and parts of Week, of Hotels in every principal Town and City in the United States and Canada.

A Work much needed by the Commercial Travellers of the Country, as well as by Hotel keepers, as a Pocket Reference or for office use.

PUBLISHED BY
JUSTUS ROE & CO.,
No. 51 CORTLANDT STREET, NEW YORK.
Corner Greenwich.

PRICE with Card, $1.50.
WITHOUT CARD, $1.00.

INTRODUCTORY.

Nature makes the tail of a horse to follow the animal; art, or common custom, has made the Preface of a book to lead it, neither are strictly necessary, or even essential, and yet while the one may be useful in switching away the flies, in fly time, the other may be equally useful for an opposite purpose, and at any time.

Nature seldom makes a blunder in any of her efforts, never| an apology; art often makes the one, and the apology that follows is generally worse than the blunder. If I have made the former in presenting this my first born to the public, it is now too late to make the latter; it is my maiden effort, and I must father the little one, trusting that by kind nursing from a generous public, it may grow in age, cast off its baby clothes, be able to sport a mustache and a cane, wear an ulster, part its hair in the middle, be a welcome guest in every household, travelling bag, or pocket, and some day be ornamental as well as useful to the world.

Common custom requires in a work of this kind a few hints, or words of advice, but for me to give advice to the great body of Commercial Travellers of our country, would be as silly as to feed a Kentucky mule, with Connecticut shoe pegs, and try to convince him that they are a new kind of oats raised in Nebraska. If any of them stand in need of that article, let them ask the first fool they meet on the street, few of them but know more than I do. And for me to advise the Hotel-keepers is almost as silly, as few of them but know better than I "how to keep a Hotel," and few of them about the country, but have received circulars and letters from me, and been bored enough already by me, in my endeavor to convince them of the advantages of a notice in my Guide, and telling them what little I know about hotel-keeping after nearly thirty years experience. To give advice is not my FORTE, I need it myself, but in view of the fact that information which cannot be relied upon is dear at any price, it has been my endeavor to give that which is perfectly reliable and trustworthy, and so meet the demand of the travelling public, let the cost be what it may.

My Guide has not been made up from Directories and the names and prices guessed at, you can guess full as well, or perhaps better than I. With the exception of the figures marked with an x, and in those cases I have heard from sources I felt to be quite trustworthy, the rates given are about the price charged, and every figure can be relied upon almost implicitly, as I have letters from the landlords in my office to show by what authority I use them, with the positive assurance from hundreds of them, that Guests with my Card will be treated with more than ordinary care and attention for the same or less pay; but the rates as they appear in my Guide, have been exclusively made to me, and are in no sense to be used as public property, or be regarded as the regular rates.

My Book is not an old face you have always perhaps been glad to welcome, but a new one, come to win its way to your favor, and its true reward. It is the little pioneer log house hotel, at the "cross roads," ready to entertain with good cheer the few guests it may now receive, and hoping some day to erect on its present site, a palatial Hotel and be able to entertain you in royal style.

All advertisements have been carefully excluded, in order to make the Guide as small as possible so as to be carried in the pocket with ease and comfort. The work will be kept standing in type, will only be issued as fast as disposed of, will be continually revised, as issued, and new Hotels, change of name or Proprietor, will be inserted as fast as received. You have only my word for this, but in this Centennial year I shall try to be as near like our great Father as I can; he couldn't tell a lie, I can, but I wont, on paper.

My Book will be sent by Mail, and Card by letter, free of Postage, on receipt of price. Books without Cards sold to all travellers. Books with Cards, sold only to Hotel keepers and Commercial Travellers.

To those who have in the past aided me, I return my hearty thanks; to those who in the future can and will do so, here's my right hand, which holds the keys to my pantry and cellar, and here's my left hand which gets hold of my pocket book first, where I carry my postage stamps and SICH.

Fraternally Yours,

JUSTUS ROE.

INSTRUCTIONS FOR USING CARD.

On the face of my Card you will perceive my request to the landlord of the Hotel whose rates appear in this Guide, and from whom I have received a letter authorizing me to use his name, rates, &c., and my signature at the bottom. On the back of the Card you must attach in your own handwriting, your name, residence, and business engaged in. On presenting yourself at the desk of a Hotel, rated in my Book where you desire accommodation, you have simply to present the Card and ask the landlord or his clerk if he recognises Mr. Roe, or the Card, if his answer is 'yes, you place your name upon the Register, which must correspond with the name upon the Card, and you will then know, by reference to the Guide, whether your stay be long or short, precisely what your bill will be.

By all means present my Card when you ask accommodation at any Hotel rated in my Guide, and distinctly remember that the rates given me are for such plain and regular accommodation as an ordinary Traveller should require, and all meals ordered out of the regular hour, or carried to rooms, fires, &c., are to be paid for extra.

For Key and instructions for using the same see Pages 118 and 119.

Alabama,	- 74	Minnesota,	-	108
Arkansas, -	- 81	Mississippi, -		- 75
California,	- 111	Missouri,	-	102
Canada, -	- 114	Nebraska, -		- 110
Colorado, -	111	Nevada,	-	110
Connecticut,	- 32	New Hampshire,	-	12
Dakota, -	110	New Jersey,	-	56
Delaware, -	- 66	New York, .		- 37
Dist. of Columbia,	67	North Carolina,		70
Florida, -	74	Ohio,	-	- 82
Georgia, -	- 72	Oregon,	-	113
Idaho, -	110	Pennsylvania,		- 59
Illinois, -	- 92	Rhode Island, -		30
Indiana, -	89	South Carolina,		- 72
Iowa, -	- 104	Tennessee,	-	80
Kansas, -	109	Texas,	-	- 77
Kentucky, -	- 78	Utah	-	111
Louisiana, -	76	Vermont, -		- 16
Maine, -	- 8	Virginia,	-	68
Maryland, -	66	West Virginia,		- 70
Massachusetts,	- 22	Wisconsin,	-	99
Michigan, -	96	Wyoming, -		- 111

MAINE

TOWN.	HOTEL.	PROPRIETOR.			
Abbott,	Abbott,	J. J. Buxton,	1.00 AI		
Addison,	Addison,	J. B. Hall,			
Alfred,	Alfred,	Richard H. Goding,			
Andover,	Andover,	Albert Thomas,			
Anson,	North Anson,	Brown & Hilton,			
Appleton,	Appleton,	Isaac Carkin,			
Athens,	Athens,	Asa C. Emery,			
Auburn,	Central,	W. H. Landers,	2.00	10	
"	Elm,	W. S. & A. Young,			
"	Maine,	O. W. Harlon,			
Augusta,	Augusta,	Marshall Whitehead			
"	Corry's,	G. A. & H. Corry,			
"	Franklin,	Alexander Smart,			
"	Mansion,	W.M.Thayer &Son,	2.00 AI	J	
Avon,	Blue Mountain,	Moses Craig, Jr.,	1.50 AB	B	
Baldwin,	West Baldwin,	Cyrus F. Burnell,			
Bangor,	Bangor,	O. M. Shaw,	2.50	14	
"	Franklin,	W. D. McLoughlin,			
"	National,	C. F. Jordan,	1.25 AD	D	12
"	P'nobscotEx'ge	A. Woodward,	2.00 AI		
Bar Harbor,	Atlantic,	J. W. Douglas,	2.50 AN	14	
Bath,	Bath,	C. M. Plummer,	1.50 AE	F	17
"	Columbian,	Chas. Dunning,			
"	Sagadahoc,	E. B. Mabury,			
"	Shannon,	Orry Shannon,			
Belfast,	American,	Tucker Bros.			
"	New England,	N. W. Holmes,			
"	Phenix,	R. G. Mitchell,			
"	Sanborn,	R. W. Mathews,	1.50 AH	C	
Belgrade,	Railroad,	Michael Connor,			

MAINE.

TOWN.	HOTEL.	PROPRIETOR.			
Benedicta,	Benedicta,	Michael Leen,	....		
Berwick,	Grant's,	Edmund Grant,	....		
Biddeford,	Biddeford,	J. C. Robbins,	....		
"	Holman's,	Daniel Holman,	....		
Blue Hill,	Hinckley's,	H. W. Hinckley,	....		
Booth Bay,	Weymouth's,	J. W. Weymouth,	....		
Bowdoinham,	Stinson,	G. W. Rideout,	1.50	AF	5 10
Bridgeton,	Cummings'	Geo. H. Cummings,	....		
"	Cumberland,	S. Tilton,	2.00	....	8 ..
Bridgewater,	Central,	J. H. Kidder,	1.50	AF	7 14
Brighton,	Walker's,	Peter Walker,	....		
Brooklin,	Brooklin,	O. W. Herrick,	....		
Brooks,	Rose's,	L. & A. H. Rose,	....		
Brunswick,	Tontine,	Sam'l B. Harman,	2.00	AJ	.. ..
Brownfield,	Brownfield,	E. T. Cotton & Son,	2.00	AG	G 16
Brownville,	Herrick's	N. C. Herrick,	....		
Bryants Pond,	Bryants Pond,	Otis Kaler,	2.00	AF	7 13
Buckfield,	Buckfield,	F.A.Warren & Son,	1.50	AF	D ..
Bucksport,	Crocker's,	W. M. Crocker,	....		
Burlington,	Page's,	Jeremiah Page,	1.50	AD	6 11
Burnham,	Clinton Gore,	Bradford Blanchard	2.00	AH	.. ..
Buxton,	Palmer's,	B. Palmer,	1.50	AF	D ..
Buxton Centre,	Cushmoc,	Sam'l Hansen & Co.	....		
Calais,	St.CroixExc'ge	Wm. H. Young,	2.00	....	7 ..
Camden,	Bay View,	J.&B.C.Adams&Co.	....		
Canaan,	Canaan,	Joseph Brown,	....		
Canton,	Central,	C. Barrow,	1.50	AD	D ..
Caribou,	Vaughn's,	W. H. Vaughn,	1.00	AB	A ..
Castine,	Hodsdon's,	Horatio E. Hodsdon	....		
China,	China,	Mrs. Chas. H. Dow,	....		
Corinna,	Corinna,	A. L. Grant,	....		
Corinth,	Warren's,	W. H. Warren,	....		
Cushing,	Hathorn's,	Samuel Hathorn,	1.00	AA	A ..
Cutler,	Cutler	I. O. Ramsdell,	....		
Dalton's,	Smith's,	Mrs.SarahF.Smith	....		
Damariscotta Mills,	Travellers,	Sanborn & Jacobs,	....		
Dedham,	Dedham,	Robert Johnson,	1.25	AD	D 14
"	Lake,	John P. Philipps,	1.25	....	7 ..
Deering,	Boardman's,	Joseph F. Boardman,	....		
Detroit,	Detroit,	Chas. Ravnes,	....		
Dexter,	Merchants Exchange	L. D. Hayes,	2.00	AI	I ..

MAINE.

TOWN.	HOTEL.	PROPRIETOR.			
Dixmount,	Mountain,	Arthur B. Piper,	1.00	AA	A ..
Dover,	Blethen's,	Wm. D. Blethen,			
Durham,	Durham,	Abner Merrill,			
East Jefferson,	Lake,	Calvin Haskell,	1.50	AH	8 ..
Eastport,	Island,	E. S. S. Kinney,	1.50	AF	7 ..
"	Passamaquoddy	Frank Fowler,	2.00	....	10 ..
Ellsworth,	American,	S. Jordan & Son,	2.00		
"	City,	W. H. Higgins & Son,	2.00	....	9 ..
"	Franklin,	B. F. Gray,	2.00	AI	J ..
Fairfield,	Fairfield,	H. & W. Sawyer,	2.00	AI	7 ..
Farmington,	Milliken's,	J. S. Milliken,			
Fort Fairfield,	Fort Fairfield,	E. N. Osborne,	1.25	AC	C ..
Foxcraft,	Jefford's,	P. M. Jeffords,			
Frankfort,	Frankfort,	D. N. Ewell,	1.50	AE	D ..
Fryeburg,	Fryeburg,	Geo. W. Abbott,	1.50	AD	D ..
Gardiner,	Evans,	Oliver C. Robbins,	2.00	AI	J ..
Garland,	Knight's,	John S. Knight,			
Gouldsboro,	Wood's,	S. G. Wood,			
Greenbush,	E.&N.A.R.R.,	N. E. Alingwood,	1.00	AC	6 ..
Greene,	Bemis',	Wm. Bemis,			
Greeneville,	Eveleth,	A. H. Walker,	2.00	AJ	J ..
Guilford,	Turner's,	Zadoc L. Turner,			
Hallowell,	Hallowell,	Horatio Q. Blake,			
Hancock,	McFarland's,	Sam'lN.McFarland	2.00	AG	G 18
Harmony,	Elm,	A. P. Bailey,	2.00	AG	5 9
Harrington,	Harrison,	Simeon Coffin,			
Harrison,	Elm,	Almond Kneeland,			
Hartland,	**Hartland,**	I. B. Littlefield,	1.50	AF	E 14
Hiram,	Mt. Cutler,	Hiram Baston,	2.00	AH	H ..
Houlton,	Exchange,	Wm. D. Buzzell,	1.50	AE	E ..
"	Snell,	W. Philbrick & Co.	2.00	AI	J ..
Jackson Brook,	Dudley,	S. H. Bosworth,	1.50	AB	B 10
Kennebunk,	Baker's,	John C. Baker,			
Kennebunkport,	Ocean Bluff,	Job Jenness & Son	3.00	A	....
Kingfield,	Franklin,	Chas. P. Lander,	1.00	....	4 ..
Kittery,	Pepperell,	E. F. Safford,	2.50	AI	I 18
La Grange,	Dirigo,	Martin Snell,			
Lee,	Elm,	J. M. True,			
Lewiston,	Lewiston,	J. B. Hill,	1.50	AF	E 15
"	Marston,	E. E. Post,	2.00	AJ	J 20
Lexington,	Somerset,	James Fillebrown,			
Liberty,	Stage,	Fred. Knowlton,	1.00	AD	5 ..
Lovell,	American,	E. W. Hill,	1.50	AF	7 ..

MAINE.

TOWN.	HOTEL.	PROPRIETOR.			
Lubec,	Cobscook,	Wm. McFadden,	1.50 AH		
Machias,	Eastern,	E. E. Stoddard,	2.00 AI		
"	Lawrence's,	S. A. Lawrence,	1.25 AD	D	10
Machiasport,	Deering,	Wm. Mitchell,	2.00 AJ	B	
Madrid,	Madrid,	Benjamin Chick,			
Manchester,	Mansion,	James Kaler,			
Masardis,	Masardis,	Joseph Pollard,			
Mat'awa'mkeag	Mat'wa'mkeag,	L.T.&G.D.Stratton	2.00 AI	B	
Mercer,	Mercer,	D. P. Stowell,	1.75 AA	A	
Mexico,	Union,	John N. Thompson,			
Milford,	Butterfield's,	Butterfield Bros.,			
Millbridge,	Atlantic,	George A. Hopkins,	2.00 AI	8	
Milo,	Oriental,	John E. Gould,	1.50 AD	D	
Monmouth,	Cochnewagin,	D. A. Pinkham,	2.00 AH	H	16
Monroe,	Durham's,	T. Durham,			
Monticello,	Monticello,	George P. Gould,			
Mt. Desert,	Hayward's,	Hayward, Brewer & Co.,	2.50 AK	14	
"	Ocean,	N. Teague & Son,	2.00 AI	I	
Mt. Vernon,	Mansion,	Loren F. Dolloff,			
Naples,	Elm,	N. A. Church,			
Newport,	Sawyer's,	Chas. Sawyer & Son,			
New Portland,	Blaisdell's,	G. C. Blaisdell,	1.50	5	
"	Canabansett,	Orlando Quint,	1.50 AF	4	
New Vineyard,	Hall's,	James Hall,			
Norridgewock,	Norridgewock,	John N. Titcomb,	1.50 AH	D	
"	Sawyer's,	I. W. Sawyer,	1.50 AH	5	
North Newry,	Poplar,	Chas. K. Bartlett,	1.50 AF	E	
Norway,	Elm,	W. W. Whitmarsh,	1.75 AC	C	
Oak Hill,	Atlantic,	S. B. Gunnison,	2.50		
Olamon,	Exchange,	G. W. Merrill,	1.25 AD	D	
Oldtown,	Codman,	E. Cousins,	2.00 AI	J	18
Old Orchard Beach,	Fiske's,	C. H. Fiske,	2.50 AJ		
"	San Souci,	Mrs.M.A.Whitten,	2.00		
Orono,	Orono,	Hugh Reed,			
Paris,	Hubbard's,	Hiram Hubbard,			
"	Union,	Horace Cummings,			
"	West Paris,	John Bicknell, Jr.,			
Parkman,	Parkman,	Thos. Seabury,			
Passadumkeag,	Exchange,	Chas. G. Folsom,			
Patten,	Patten,	Chas. L. Hackett,			
Pembroke,	Pembroke,	Joseph P. Rogers,			

TOWN.	HOTEL.	PROPRIETOR.	
Phillips,	Elmwood,	E. D. Prescott,	1.75 AA A ..
Pittsfield,	Fletcher's,	Geo. H. Fletcher,	... ...
Porter,	Porter,	Moses N. Stanley,	... ...
Portland,	City,	J. K. Martin,	2.50 AJ 10 ..
"	Cumberland,	N. C. Pinkham,	1.00 AA A ..
"	Falmouth,	L. Stevens,	3.50 AR P ..
"	Groton,	F. M. Sawyer,	1.25 .... 7 ..
"	Perry's,	J. G. Perry,	2.00 AI I ..
"	Preble,	M. S. Gibson & Co.	... ...
"	St. Julian,	George E. Ward,	1.00 EG .. ..
"	United States,	T. Wolcott & Co.,	2.00 AJ I ..
Presque Isle,	Presque Isle,	Geo. F. Whitney,	... ...
Princeton,	Princeton,	Gardner Lovering,	... ...
Raymond,	Central,	W. H. Smith,	1.75 AG G ..
Readfield,	Elmwood,	V. Stearns,,	2.00 .... 10 ..
"	Hutchinson's,	J. J. Hutchinson,	2.00 AF B ..
Rockland,	Thorndike,	Kallock & White,	2.50 .... 15 ..
Rumford,	Rumford,	A. H. Price,	2.00 .... 11 ..
Saco,	New Old Orchard,	E.C.Staples & Son,	4.00 AR .. ..
Saccarappa,	Presumpscott,	Mrs. E. M. Pratt,	1.00 .... 5 ..
Scarboro,	Gunnison's,	S. B. Gunnison,	... ...
Searsport,	Searsport,	Wm.H.Mathew's,	... ...
Sebec,	Sebec,	Oakman Durgan,	1.50 AF .. ..
Sedgewick,	Travellers Home	D. P. Dority,	1.50 .... 6 ..
Sherman,	Jackman's,	E. A. Jackman,	... ...
Shirley,	Shirley,	John Randall,	... ...
Skowhegan,	Elm,	Thos. H. Springer,	1.50 AF E ..
"	Turner,	Wm. G. Hezelton,	2.00 AI J ..
Somerville,	Union,	W. W. Jones,	... ...
S. Thomaston,	Forest	Geo. C. Dow,	1.00 AC B ..
S. Waterford,	Pine Grove,	Dudley Bros.,	1.25 AD D ..
Springfield,	Springfield,	A. D. Clark,	... ...
Springvale,	Tebbetts',	S. D. Tebbetts,	2.00 .... 9 ..
Standish,	Standish,	Chas. Thompson,	... ...
Strong,	Exchange,	Wm. McKeen,	... ...
S. W. Harbor,	Freeman's	James R. Freeman,	... ...
Thomaston,	Georges,	Wm. K. Bickford,	2.00 AG G 16
"	Knox,	A. C. Delano,	2.00 ... .
Topsfield,	Stage,	E. Lovering,	... ...
Turner,	TravellersHome	Calvin McKenney,	... ...
Union,	Rural,	Wm. E. Cobb,	... ...
Unity,	Centre,	Thos.J.Whitehouse	... ...
Upton,	Abbott's,	Wm. I. Abbott,	... ...

MAINE.

TOWN.	HOTEL.	PROPRIETOR.		
Van Buren,	Van Buren,	M. C. Hall,	1.00	A A A ..
Vassalboro,	Murray's,	Wm. Murray,	1.50	A E E ..
Veazie,	Everitt,	A. B. Waters,	1.50	A F D ..
Waldoboro,	Medomack,	John D. Miller,		....
Waltham,	Waltham,	Wm. M. Fox,		....
Warren,	Jones'	John Jones,		....
Waterboro,	Union,	John C. Durgin,	1.50	A F C ..
Waterville,	Williams,	A. O. Smith,	2.00	A J 10 ..
Wayne,	Wayne,	Stillman L. Howard	1.50	A D D 14
Wells,	Highland Cottage,	Charles Perkins,	1.25	.... 7 ..
W. Farmington,	Elm,	Wm. F. Cilley,	1.50	A I 5 9
Weston,	S. Weston,	John Weller,		....
W. Waterville,	Bacon's,	A. D. Bacon,		....
Wilton,	Franklin,	J. C. Miller,	1.50	A E 5 ..
Windham,	Pleasant River,	J. B. Morrell,	1.25	A D D ..
Winn,	Katahdin,	S. B. Gates,	2.00	A I 5 ..
Winthrop,	Winthrop,	E. Getchell,		....
Winterport,	Commercial,	C. R. & S. Merrill,	2.00	A I 7 ..
Wiscassett,	Belle Haven,	Sam'l B. Erskine,	2.00	A I I ..
York,	Marshall's,	Marshall Bros.,		....
"	Sea Cottage,	Charles A. Grant,	2.00	A I I ..

NEW-HAMPSHIRE.

TOWN.	HOTEL.	PROPRIETOR.		
Alstead,	Burge's,	F. J. Burge,		....
Alton,	New Alton,	J. H. Fifield,	2.00	A I I ..
Alton Bay,	Winnipisogee,	A.O. Phillipps & Co.	2.50	A 15 ..
Amherst,	Amherst,	Thomas Saunders,		....
Ashuelot,	Ashuelot,	Stephen O. Hawkins,		....
Ashland,	Squan Lake,	James M. Cotten,	2.00	A I I 16
Barnsted,	American,	S.G.Shackford&S'n	2.00	A F E 14
Bartlett,	Bartlett,	Frank George,		....
" Lower,	East Branch,	W. M. & A. Pitman,	2.00	A F E ..
Belmont,	American,	C. D. Bryant,		....
"	Belmont,	Ira Mooney,	1.00	A F 6 ..
Berlin,	Mt. Forest,	M. C. FOREST,	1.50	A D D 14
Bethlehem,	Winch's,	S. F. Winch,		....
Boscawen,	National,	S. A. Ambrose,		....
Bradford,	Fitts',	J. M. Fitts,		....
Brookline,	Davis',	Marshall Davis,		....
Campton,	Silver's,	Albert W. Silver,		....

NEW-HAMPSHIRE. 13

NAME.	HOTEL.	PROPRIETOR.			
Canaan,	East Canaan,	James Stevens,			
Candia,	Union,	Geo. W. Robinson,			
Centre Harbor,	Emery's,	Smith F. Emery,			
"	Senter,	J. L. Huntress,			
Charlestown,	CheshireBridge	Lovell Bros.,	1.25 AD B		..
"	Dinsmore's,	J. B. Dinsmore,			
Chester,	Village,	D. L. Batchelder,	1.50 AH E 14		
Chesterfield,	Prospect,	J. W. Herrick,	2.00 AJ	8	14
"	Spaffords',	Sanford Gurnsey,	1.25	....	7 ..
Claremont,	Sullivan,	James Leet,	2.00 AI	..	..
"	Tremont,	A. F. Pierce & Co.,	2.00 AIF		..
Colebrook,	Dix,	George Parsons,	3.00	....	14 ..
"	Monadnock,	Thomas G. Rowan,	1.50 A		7 ..
Concord,	American,	D. G. Marsh,			
"	Eagle,	John A. White,	3.00 AL	..	..
"	Elm,	Geo. F. Bean,	1.50	....	8 ..
"	Phenix,	W. S. Baker,			
Conway,	Conway,	L. H. Eastman,	2.00 AI	I	..
Cornish,	Ryan's,	W. P. Ryan,			
Croydon,	Sargent's,	David A. Sargent,			
Deerfield,	Page's,	George Page,			
Deering,	Appleton's,	Jas. M. Appleton,			
Derby,	Railroad,	Alden B. Smith,			
Dover,	American,	D. C. Wiggins,			
"	Chase's,	James F. Chase,			
"	Dover Point,	J. Spinney,			
"	Kimball,	Charles E. Smith,			
"	New England,	John A. Smith,			
"	NewHam'shire	Wm. Walker,			
"	United States,	J. A. Hoye,			
East Jaffray,	Riverside,	H. B. Wheeler,	1.50 AF F		..
Eaton,	Robertson's,	H. H. Robertson,			
Enfield,	Clark's,	G. W. Clark,			
Enfield Centre,	Montcalm,	John H. Morse,	1.50 AD D 14		
Epping,	Pawtuckaway,	Wm. R. Bunker,	1.50 AH	7	..
Erroll,	Akers',	John Akers,			
"	Erroll,	W. W. Bragg,	1.50 AC D		..
Exeter,	Hoyt's,	T. B. Hoyt,			
"	Squamscotts,	A. P. Blake,	2.00 AI	I	..
Factory Village,	Belmont,	Ira Mooney,	1.00 AF	6	12
Farmington,	Varney's,	Stephen F. Varney,			
Fitzwilliam,	Fitzwilliam,	Newt'n&Batchellers			
"	Gage's, S. R.	A. Gage,	1.00	....	7 ..
Francestown,	Francestown,	Wm. H. Farnum,			

NEW-HAMPSHIRE.

TOWN.	HOTEL.	PROPRIETOR.			
Franconia,	Lafayette,	Joel Spooner & Son,	2.00 AI	I	..
Franklin,	Franklin,	A. K. Moore,	1.50 A	7	..
"	Webster,	O. B. Davis,	2.00 AI	...	..
Freedom,	Carroll,	G. Fowle,	1.50 AH	6	10
Gilmantown,	Marsh's,	Isaac C. Marsh,	...	...	..
Goffstown,	New Ham'shire	Wm. Cunningham,	1.25 AI	6	10
Gorham,	Gorham,	Jas. A. Callahan,	2.00 AI	I	..
"	Milliken's,	W. & C. R. Milliken,	...	...	..
Grafton,	Pleasant Valley	Martin S. Williams,	...	...	..
Great Falls,	Grant's,	Edmund Grant,	...	...	..
"	Pearl's,	Ichabod Pearl,	...	...	..
Greenfield,	Dunklee's,	H. H. Denklee,	...	...	..
Greenland,	Brackett's,	George E. Brackett,	1.00 AF	7	..
Hampton,	Union,	Otis F. Whittier,	2.00 AI	I	..
Hampton Beach,	Dumas',	S. H. Dumas,	...	...	..
"	Leavitt's,	T. & J. Leavitt,	...	...	..
"	Whittier's,	O. H. Whittier,	...	...	..
"	Yeaton's,	Phillip Yeaton,	...	...	..
Hancock,	Eaton's,	John F. Eaton,	1.25 AD	D	..
Hanover,	Dartmouth,	Horace Frary,	...	...	..
Haverhill,	Metcalf's,	Parker Metcalf,	1.50 A	5	..
"	Smith's,	Charles G. Smith,	2.00 AI	...	..
Hebron,	Central,	Fred Clement,	...	...	..
Heniker,	Craig's,	John S. Craig,	...	...	..
"	National,	John Mussey	2.00	7	..
Hinsdale,	Ashuelot,	H. M. Slate,	2.00 AI	I	14
Hopkinstown,	Contoocook,	Charles E. Taylor,	...	...	..
Jackson,	Wentworth's,	M. C. Wentworth,	...	...	..
Jaffrey,	Cutter's, S. R.	Jonas Cutter,	1.50 AI	...	..
Jefferson,	Maple's,	Mrs. M. H. Bowles,	2.00 AH	8	..
"	Waumbeck,	Wm. P. Merrill,	3.00 AKK		..
Keene,	City,	L. W. Cummings,	2.00 AI	J	..
"	Cheshire,	M. J. Sherman,	2.50	14	..
"	Eagle,	A. R. Mason,	2.00 AI	G	15
Kingston,	Alpha,	E. M. Frost,	2.00 AH	...	..
Laconia,	Laconia,	Elkins Bros.,	2.00 AI	I	14
Lake Village,	Belknap,	David B. Storey,	...	...	..
Lancaster,	American,	F. Richardson & Co.	2.00	7	..
"	Lancaster,	B. H. Corning,	...	...	..
Lebanon,	Lafayette,	A. A. Hall,	2.00 AI	6	..
Lisbon,	Moore's,	Azariah W. Moore,	...	...	..
Littleton,	Jennison's,	Mrs. Wm. Jennison,	...	...	..
London,	Cutchin's,	M. C. Cutchins,	...	...	..
Lyme,	Pavillion,	John S. Kent,	...	...	..

NEW-HAMPSHIRE. 15

TOWN.	HOTEL.	PROPRIETOR.			
Manchester,	Amoskeag,	Michael Linen,	...	...	...
"	City,	F. A. McLAUGHLIN,	2.00	AI	I ..
"	Haseltine's,	P. W. Hazeltine,	2.00	AJ	I ..
"	Manchester,	Wm. Shepard,	...	...	...
"	Massabesic,	J. B. Hill & Sons,	...	...	...
"	Merrimac,	Benjamin Callam,	...	...	...
"	National,	J. H. Willey,	2.00	....	9 ..
"	Waverly,	Ira A. Moore,	...	...	...
Marlow,	Forest,	Henry H. Huntley,	1.50	AD	D ..
"	Jones',	Edmund Jones,	1.50	AE	H ..
Merrimac,	Merrimac,	H. N. Colston,	2.00	AH	6 ..
Milford,	Union,	H. L. Barnard,	2.00	AI	I ..
Milton Three Ponds,	Tri-Mountain,	J. R. Horne,	1.50	AF	D 13
Moultonboro,	Union,	Aug. P. Jacklard	1.50	AC	C 12
Mt. Vernon,	Bellevue,	J. H. A. Bruce,	2.00	AH	F ..
Nashua,	Tremont,	Gilman Script're	2.50	AK	L ..
"	Willards,	Charles Willard,	...	...	...
New Castle,	Wentworth S.R.	Campbell & Jewett	3.00	AN	N ..
New Ipswich,	Clark's,	Peter Hobart Clark,	2.00	AH	H ..
"	Wheeler,	B. Sawyer & Son,	...	...	...
New London,	Seamans',	D. S. Seamans,	...	...	...
New Market,	Silver's,	Joseph B. Silver,	2.00	AI	.. ..
Newport,	Phenix,	Jas. H. Brown,	2.00	AI	I ..
"	Putney's,	E. L. Putney,	...	...	...
Newton,	Trav'ler's Home	George W. Hoyt,	1.25	AF	D 13
North Conway,	Eastman's	Alfred Eastman,	2.00	A	11 ..
"	N. Conway,	N. R. Mason,	2.50	A	11 ..
"	Washingt'n, SR	James M. Gibson,	2.50	AF	F ..
North Stratford,	Hinman's,	H. B. Hinman,	...	...	...
Northwood,	Brown's,	Edward C. Brown,	...	...	...
Orford,	Orford,	John L. Hazeltine,	2.00	AH	G ..
Ossippee,	Carroll,	Elisha P. Allen,	1.00	....	7 ..
Peterboro,	French's,	Henry K. French,	2.00	AI	I ..
"	St. James,	Munroe A. Smith,	1.00	A	.. ..
Pittsfield,	Washington,	Thomas B. Tucker,	2.50	AL	H ..
Plymouth,	Plymouth,	Buchanan & Willis,	2.00	AHH	..
Portsmouth,	Franklin,	G. H. Atkins,	1.50	AF	F ..
"	Kearsage,	James E. Dennett,	2.50	AJ	J 21
"	National,	J. C. Perkins,	2.00	....	..
"	Rockingham,	Frank W. Hilton,	3.50	AM	N ..
Raymond,	Bean's,	Frank G. Bean,	...	...	...
Rochester,	Dodge's,	P. Thorne Dodge,	...	...	...
"	Mansion,	S. H. Wentworth,	2.00	AHH	..
Rumney,	Jones',	Greenleaf C. Jones,	...	...	...

NEW HAMPSHIRE.

TOWN.	HOTEL.	PROPRIETOR.			
Rye,	Philbrook's,	Mrs. J.C. Philbrook,			
Salem,	Salem,	Albert L. Armor.	1.25	AC	C
Seabrook,	Washington,	John H. Parker,			
So. NewMarket,	Elm,	Ann M. Wiggins,	1.00		5
Stoddard,	**Harding's**	Otis H. Harding,	1.50	AE	D
Strafford,	Peavey's,	John C. Peavey,			
Suncook,	Pembroke,	Poore & Parshley,	2.00	AH	G
Tamworth,	Gilman's,	Joseph H. Gilman,			
Temple,	Central,	James Woodward,	1.50	AF	7
Tilton,	Dexter,	J. L. Coffin,			
Troy,	Monadnock,	J. Clement,			
Union,	**Union,**	Robert H. Pike,	2.00	AG	G
Wakefield,	Wakefield,	Mrs. G.H. Wiggin,			
Walpole,	Wentworth,	Horace A. Perry,	2.00	AH	H
Warner,	Warner,	M. C. Bartlett,			
Weare,	N. Weare,	Abner P. Collins,			
Wentworth,	Smith's,	Eleazer Smith,			
West Lebanon,	Southworth,	E. G. Southworth,	1.50	AF	D
Westmoreland,	Valley,	Holland Bennett,			
West Ossippee,	Plummer's,	James H. Plummer,			
Wilton,	Center's,	Sam'l N. Center,			
Winchester,	Winchester,	E. C. Richards,	2.00		12
Wolfboro,	Lake,	Geo. Keniston,	2.00	A	10
"	Peavey's,	John L. Peavey,			
Woodsville,	Parker's,	E. G. Parker,	2.00	AI	7

VERMONT.

TOWN.	HOTEL.	PROPRIETOR.			
Albany,	Darling's,	J. B. Darling,			
"	Howard's,	W. Howard,			
Alburgh.	Albu'h Springs,	E. H. Hudson,			
"	Ames',	Geo. W. Ames,			
"	Mansion,	Chauncey Smith,			
Arlington,	Arlington,	A. Bartlett,			
Bakersfield,	Beales',	E. H. Beale,			
Barnard,	Silver Lake,	C. E. French,			
Barnet,	Nillson,	L. W. Hazelton,	1.50	AH	7 13
Barre,	Barre Spring,	S. Bruce,			
"	**Cottage,**	S. R. ORDWAY,	2.00	AI	I
"	Twingville,	H. Peck,			
Barton,	Crystal Lake,	V. N. Spaulding,	2.00	AI	7
Barton Landing,	Valley,	C. W. Cade,	1.50	AF	5 9

VERMONT.

TOWN.	HOTEL.	PROPRIETOR.		
Bellows Falls,	Island,	S. C. Flemming,		
"	Towns',	Charles Towns,		
Bennington,	Gates',	John R. Gates,		
"	Stark,	Wm. H. Cady,		
"	Walloomsac,	Alfred Robinson,	2.50 A	14 ..
Benson,	Union,	Jonas Reid,		
Bolton,	Bolton,	R. E. Weller,		
Bradford,	Trotten,	H. E. Harris,		
Braintree,	Snowville,	Nath. Hutchinson,		
Brandon,	Brandon,	Vail & Merritt,	2.50 AJ	I 16
Brattleboro,	American,	G. A. Boyden,	2.00	11 ..
"	Brooks',	Chas. G. Lawrence,		
"	Revere,	H. C. Nash,		
Bridgewater,	Carpenter's,	C. B. Carpenter,	1.50 AF	6 10
Bridport,	Bridport,	N. B. Phelps,	2.00 AI	9 ..
Bristol,	Bristol,	J. J. Ridley,		
Brookfield,	Traveller's,	Mrs. E. Clark,		
Brownington,	Central,	J. A. Wyman,		
Burlington,	American,	H. H. Howe,		
"	Park,	H. F. Pettingill,		
"	Rowe's,	R. C. ROWE,	2.00....	10 ..
"	Van Ness,	D. C. Barber & Co.,	3 00AL ..	..
Cabot,	Winooski,	Wm. P. Whittier,	2.00 AH	A ..
Calais,	Moscow,	A. Slayton,		
Cambridge,	Borough,	C. B. Waite,	2.00 AE	E ..
Canaan,	Canaan,	Charles H. Weeks,		
Castleton,	Sanford,	Franklin Sanford,		
Charleston,	Clyde River,	A. J. Morrill,		
Charlotte,	Washington,	O. H. Alexander,	1.75 AH	H ..
Chelsea,	Orange County,	A. W. Whitney,		
Chester,	Central,	N. O. Johnson,	2.00 AI	I ..
"	Chester,	H. H. Ingraham,		
Clarendon Spr.,	Clarendon,	B. Murray & Sons,	2.50 AK	K ..
"	Green Mount'n,	A. F. Style,		
Concord,	Concord,	A. W. Houghton,		
Corinth,	Foster's,	L. P. Foster,		
Coventry,	Coventry,	E. W. Landgmayd,		
Craftsburg,	Orleans,	Wm. Hodgen,		
Cattingsville,	Todd's,	Horace Todd,		
Danby,	Danby & Mt. Tabor,	W. H. Bond,	2.00 AI	I ..
Danville,	Smith's,	A. H. Smith,		
Derby Centre,	Central,	W. H. Hinman,	2.00 AF	F ..
Derby Line,	Derby Line,	H. B. Benson,		

TOWN.	HOTEL.	PROPRIETOR.		
Dorset,	East Dorset,	B. Barrows,		
"	North Dorset,	John Curtis,		
"	Washington,	George W. Baker,	1.50	9..
Dover,	West Dover,	A. B. Collins,		
Drummerstown,	Frink's,	S. W. Frink,		
East Arlington,	Green Mount'n,	N. G. Hard,	1.50 AD	D 13
Eden,	Eden,	Jacob Harrington,	1.00 A	5..
"	Eden Pond,	Isaac D. Davis,		
Elmore,	Daniels',	S. Daniels,		
Enosburgh,	Eagle,	F. C. Kimball, Jr.,	2.00 AG	G..
Essex Junction,	Central,	Fred W. Chase,	2.00 AI	10..
"	Junction,	Samuel Tyler,		
Factory Point,	Colburns',	John S. Angel,	1.50 A	7..
"	Thayers',	H. W. Davis,		
Fairfax,	Fairfax,	A. Foss,	2.00 AH	7..
"	Valley,	E. J. Pease,	1.50 AG	D..
Fairfield,	Driscoll's,	J. G. Driscoll,		
E. "	Isham's,	S. Isham & Son,	1.00 A	5..
Fair Haven,	Knights',	C. C. Knight,	2.00 AI	I 16
Felchville,	Felchville,	Gilbert A. Davis,	1.75 AE	E 14
Ferrisburg,	Martin's,	S. Martin,		
Franklin,	Franklin,	Herbert S. Chaplin,	2.00 AH	5..
Georgia,	Depot,	P. E. Spencer,		
"	Franklin,	R. S. Shepard,		
Glover,	Union,	Ethan E. Foster,		
Grafton,	Phelps',	F. & H. Phelps,	1.25 AH	7..
Granville,	Granville,	D. W. Rogers,	2.00 AF	F..
Greensboro,	Greensboro,	Anson B. Cook,		
Guilford,	Broad Brook,	Chauncey Guellow,	1.50 AE	B..
"	Springs,	C. C. Lynde,		
Guildhall,	Essen,	Wm. H. Hartshorn,		
Halifax,	Stark's,	Jedediah Stark,		
Hancock,	Green Mount'n,	John E. Wright,		
Hardwick,	E. Hardwick,	Drennon Bros.		
"	Hardwick,	John Birks,	2.00 AI	I..
Hartford.	Union,	H. M. Cutting,		
"	White River,	Charles W. Pease,	2.00 AI	I..
Hartland,	Pavillion,	R. L. Britton,	2.00 AI	I..
"	Railroad,	Frank Dunton,		
Highgate,	Champlain,	J. Osborne,		
"	Green Mount'n,	W. H. Lantman,	1.50	6..
"	Stinehouse,	Misses Stinehouse,		

VERMONT.

TOWN.	HOTEL.	PROPRIETOR.		
Hinesburg,	Flanagan's,	Geo. W. Flanagan,	1.50 AF	F ..
Hubbardton,	Webster's,	Martin J. Webster,	1.00 AF	A ..
Huntington,	Camel's Hump	G. Conger,		
"	Huntington,	E. T. Collins,		
Hyde Park,	American,	E. B. Sawyer,		
"	Union,	D. Randall,		
"	Valley,	Poteus Butts,		
Irasburgh,	Irasburg,	E. W. Powell,		
Jamaica,	Jamaica,	S. E. Rawson,		
Jericho,	Barney's,	M. Barney,		
Johnson,	Johnson,	G. H. Saxby,	2.00 AH	D ..
Jonesville,	Forest,	A. B. Cooper,		
Landgrave,	Green Mount'n,	David Howard,		
Larrabies Point,	United States,	Fant & Kimball,		
LeicesterJunc'n	Junction,	O. C. Huntley,	2.00 AF	E ..
Lowell,	Mt. Morris,	H. C. Brown,	1.00 A	4 ..
Ludlow,	Ludlow,	H. A. Green,	2.00	8 ..
Lunenburgh,	Chandler's,	J. B. S. Chandler,	2.00 AH	F ..
Lynden,	Lynden,	S. R. McGaffey,		
"	Lynden Centre,	C. E. Hoffman,		
"	Walker's,	George B. Walker,		
Manchester,	Elm, S. R.	Chas. F. Orvis,	2.50 AJ	....
"	Equinox,	F. H. Orvis,	4.00 AQ	25 ..
Marshfield,	Eagle,	L. D. Bemis,	1.25 A	7 ..
Middlebury,	Addison,	Darwin Rider,		
"	**Glen,**	WILL ALLEN & CO.,	1.50	10 ..
"	Middlebury,	T. B. Smith,		
Middlesex,	Washington,	Benjamin Barrett,		
Middletown,	Montvert,	D. Doolittle,		
"	Valley,	Orlando Gates,	2.00	7 ..
Milton,	Austin,	A. N. Austin,	2.00 AI	I 18
"	Elm Tree,	Wm. Landon,		
"	The Rest,	J. D. Gale,		
Monkton,	Collins',	Elmer D. Collins,		
Montgomery,	Sampson's,	A. S. Sampson,		
Montpelier,	**American,**	C. CLARK,	2.00 AH	H 18
"	Bishop's,	H. H. Bishop,		
"	Pavillion,	T. O. Bailey,	3.00 A	....
"	Union,	George P. Foster,	2.00	10 ..
Moretown,	Village,	Noah Fisher,		
Morrisville,	Morrisville,	Orcutt & Boynton,		
Newberry,	Spring,	R. W. Chamberlin,		
New Haven,	New Haven,	Wm. M. Patch,		

VERMONT.

TOWN.	HOTEL.	PROPRIETOR.			
Newport,	Bellevue,	Horace Bean,	2.50	....	15 ..
"	Memphremagog	W. F. Bowman	...	...	...
Newport,	Newport,	N. C. Cole,	2.00	AF	F 15
NewportCentre	Spring,	A. R. Glines,	...	...	...
Northfield,	National,	William Blood,	...	...	...
"	**Northfield,**	J. H. RANSOM,	2.00	....	8 ..
North Wolcott,	North Wolcott.	A. B. Pike,	1.50	AE	5 ..
Norwich,	Union,	N. F. Bush,	...	...	...
Orwell,	Boynton,	Joshua W. Boynton,	...	...	...
Pawlet,	Franklin,	D. W. Bromley,	...	...	...
"	Indian River,	D. Woodward,	...	...	...
Peacham,	Atwell's,	John Atwell,	...	...	...
Peru,	Bromleys,	G. K. Davis,	1.50	A	7 ..
Pittsfield,	GreenMountain	J. H. Spaulding,	1.25	....	6 ..
Pittsford,	Otter Creek,	L. F. Schofield,	...	...	...
Plainfield,	Plainfield,	B. P. Young,	...	...	...
"	Spring,	James Morse,	...	...	...
Plymouth,	Tyson,	Eugene O. Pratt,	2.00	AG	G 16
"	Union,	L. J. Green,	...	...	...
"	Wilder House,	D. P. Wilder,	1.50	AD	D ..
Post Mills,	Lake,	Nathan Davis,	...	...	...
Poultney,	Beaman's,	C. C. Beaman,	2.00	AE	E 13
"	Eagle,	A. Murdock,	...	...	...
"	Poultney,	E. G. Dyer,	...	...	...
Pownall,	Union,	L. Burlingame,	...	...	...
Putney.	Kendrick's,	D. H. Kendrick,	1.50	AF	....
Readsboro,	Stowe,	Carp'nter&Faulkn'r	...	...	...
Richford,	American,	J. B. Sweatland,	...	...	...
"	Union,	J. P. Goddard,	...	...	...
Richmond,	Richmond,	L. Love,	...	...	...
Rochester,	Rochester,	T. M. Eaton & Co.	1.50	AE	8 ..
Roxbury,	Summit,	James P. Warner,	...	...	...
Royalton,	Cascadnac,	John G. Lessure,	2.00	AI	7 ..
Rutland,	Bates',	Paige & Tolhurst,	...	...	...
"	Bardwell,	J. W. Crampton,	...	...	...
"	**Berwick,**	C. F. RICHARDSON,	2.00	AI	G ..
"	Central,	J.A.Salisbury&Co.,	...	...	...
"	Farmers',	J. E. Johnson,	...	...	...
Salisbury,	Salisbury,	Rollin T. Howard,	1.00	AB	A ..
"	Lake Dunmore,	Hitchcock&Porter,	...	...	...
Saxton's River,	Saxton's River,	M. A. Wilder,	...	...	...
Sheffield,	Sheffield,	N. L. Folsom,	...	...	...
Shelburne,	La Platte,	W. A. Weed,	...	...	...

TOWN.	HOTEL.	PROPRIETOR.	
Sheldon,	Bellevue,	A. H. Keith,	
"	Central,	S. Vanderburgh,	
"	Kettele,	J. C. Kettele,	
"	Landon,	Wm. Landon,	
"	Portland,	D. Wright,	
"	Valley,	A. C. Wheeler,	
Sherburne,	Sherburne,	B. Maxham,	
Shoreham,	Shoreham,	Bennett & Jones,	
South Royalton,	South Royalton	Woodward & Son,	2.00 .... 8 ..
South Hero,	Island,	C. S. Keeler,	
"	Iodine Spring.	W. Corbin,	1.50 AF F ..
South Troy,	Waumbec,	A. Hodsden,	2.00 AG F ..
Springfield,	Springfield,	George O. Henry,	
St. Albans,	American,	G. M. Pierce,	
"	Central,	J. P. Corry,	
"	St. Albans,	WILLARD PIERCE,	2.00 .... 10 ..
"	Tremont,	T. Brennen,	
"	Welden,	T. Lavender,	
St. Johnsbury,	Avenue,	Howe & Morrison,	2.00 AHH ..
"	St. Johnsbury,	T. B. Lyford,	2.50 AK ....
Stamford,	Wilmarth,	A. W. Wilmarth,	
Starksboro,	Green Mount'n,	J. Kinsley,	
Stratton,	Stratton,	Mrs. F. Wyman & Son	
Sudbury,	Hyde's,	A. W. Hyde, Jr.,	
"	Royal,	Royal W. Pitts,	
Sutton,	Sutton,	R. Jenness,	
Swanton,	Central,	C. F. Smith,	
"	Barney,	T. F. Bolac,	1.50 AH E ..
Topsham,	Wait's River,	A. Worthen,	
Townsend,	Dunham's,	J. Dunham & Son,	
Underhill,	Dixon S. R.	L. M. Dixon,	2.00 AF F ..
Underhill Cent'e	Pronty's,	L. O. Horton,	
Vergennes,	American,	E. C. Everest,	
"	Cataract,	Hayes & Wright,	
"	Franklin,	J. W. Pitts,	2.00 .... 8 ..
"	Stevens,	D. McBride & Co.,	
Vernon,	Burrows',	J. F. Burrows,	
Waitsfield,	Waitsfield,	Wm. Dodge,	
Walden,	Dutton's,	A. E. Dutton,	
"	Rogers',	B. A. Rogers,	
Wallingford,	Wallingford,	E. C. Barrows,	
Warren,	Warren,	H. W. Lyford,	
Washington,	Washington,	J. Colburn,	

VERMONT.

TOWN.	HOTEL.	PROPRIETOR.	
Waterbury,	Village,	Mrs. Nancy F. Brown	....
"	Waterbury,	Lester S. Hills,	....
Waterford,	Valley,	H. A. Bowman,	....
Waterville,	Mount'nSpring	S. R. Miller,	1.50 AF E ..
Wells River,	Coosuck,	Durant & Adams,	....
"	Lake St. Catharines,	Charles W. Potter,	....
"	Union Hall,	H. Lewis,	....
West Burke,	Trull's,	David Trull,	2.00 AI I 16
West Concord,	West Concord,	J. C. Spencer,	1.50 AF 7 ..
West Fairlee,	Eagle,	Fred W. Farnham,	2.00 AF F 15
West Rutland,	Barnes',	John H. Hazelton,	....
Weybridge,	Otter Creek,	H. Tyler,	....
Wheelock,	Cal'doniaSpring	John W. Sanborn,	2.00 AHH ..
Williamstown,	Gulf Spring,	George W. Lang,	1.25 AF D 14
Williamsville,	Williamsville,	S. W. Bowker,	....
Wilmington,	Vermont,	Wilder & Kidder,	1.50 AH F ..
Windsor,	Ascutney,	C. O. Durkee,	2.00 AG 7 10
"	Dudley,	Mrs. Geo. Dudley,	....
"	Windsor,	J. H. Simmonds,	....
Winhall,	Green Mount'n,	W. F. Mills,	....
Wolcott,	Wolcott,	L. A. Tillotson,	1.50 A 8 ..
Woodstock,	Eagle,	C. A. Fairbanks,	....
Worcester,	Worcester,	A. A. Bliss,	1.50 AF 5 ..

MASSACHUSETTS.

TOWN.	HOTEL.	PROPRIETOR.	
N. Abington,	Culver's	J. W. Culver,	2.00 AH F ..
Adams,	Arnold	Streeter, Smith & Co.,	....
North Adams,	Ballou's	M. Ballou & Sons,	2.00 AI 13 21
"	Bradley's	Mrs. M. B. Bradley,	2.00 x ...
South Adams,	Daniels'	A. D. Daniels,	2.00 .... 10 ..
Amesbury,	American	Sarah Kimball,	2.00 x ...
Amherst,	Amherst	N. S. Beebe,	2.50 AK L ..
"	Parker's	Geo. Parker,	....
Andover,	Carter's	Chas. L. Carter,	2.00 x ...
"	Elm	George H. Bean,	2.00 AI 11 14
Arlington,	Arlington	Chas. S. Jacobs,	2.00 x ...
Ashburnham,	Central	W. R. Adams,	....
Ashfield,	Ashfield	Allen Philipps,	2.00 x ...
Ashland,	Scott's	Wm. A. Scott & Son,	....
Athol,	Athol	Albert Miller,	2.00 AI J ..
"	Summit	D. A. Jennison,	2.00 AH G ..

MASSACHUSETTS.

TOWN.	HOTEL.	PROPRIETOR.		
Attleboro,	Ryder's	J. G. Ryder,	2-00	.... 10 ..
Ayer,	Beverley's	Luke Beverly,	....	....
"	Smith's	George J Smith,	....	....
"	Spencer's	J. B. Spencer,	, ...	....
Baldwinsville,	Narragansett	George Partridge,	1.50 A F	7 ..
Barnstable,	Globe	E. H. Eldridge,	2.00 AI	F ..
Barre,	Massasoit	John F. Brooks,	2.00 A E	E ..
"	Naquag	C. A. Clapp,	2.00 A G	D ..
Bedford,	Bedford	Frank B. Holden,	....	....
Belchertown,	Belchertown	Willard C. Owen,	2.00 x	.. ..
Berlin,	Carter's	C. Carter,	2.00 x	.. ..
Blackstone,	Union	A. A. Wheelock,	....	....
Boston.				
371 Wash'n St.	Adams	D. Chamberlin,	....	....
56 Hanover,	American	Lewis Rice & Son,	3.00	....
Causeway & Canal,	Arlington	S. H. Dumas,	2.50 AI	I 20
129 Dorchester Avenue,	Avenue	Thos. Leavitt,	1.50	.... 8 ..
Boylston & Clarendon,	The Brunswick	J. W. Wolcott,	4.50	....
523 Tremont,	Clarendon	J. Pickering Draper	3.50 AP	P ..
68 Causeway,	Commercial	Chas. F. Clark,	2.00 AI	J ..
Washington & Springfield,	Commonwealth	J. W. Wolcott,	4.00 :	....
391 Wash'gt'n,	Marlboro	N. B. Stevens,	3.00	.... 15 ..
17 Brattle,	Marston's	R. Marston & Co.,	0.75 ED	.. ..
347 Wash'gt'n,	Milliken's	F. Milliken,	2.00 AJ	J ..
"	"	"	0.50 E	.. ..
44 Portland,	Montreal	Otis C. Merrill,	1.50 EJ	7 ..
Brattle Sq.,	Quincy	Bell & Johnson,	2.50 AL	.. ..
Court Sq.,	Sherman	Barney Hull,	1.00 EG	.. ..
Tremont cor.. Beacon,	Tremont	Chapin Gurney & Co.	....	....
Beach cor. Lincoln,	United States	Barnes, Gill & Co.,	3.50 AR	P ..
15 Howard,	Washington	A. W. Barker,	1.00 A	7 ..
Paris & Sumner,	Webster	A. D. Jaquith,	1.25 AC	E ..
34 Bowdoin,	Winthrop	J. R. Bassett, Agt.	2.50 AK	K ..
Court Ave.,	Young's	Geo. Young,	1.00 E	.. ..
Bradford,	Knowles'	David C. Knowles,	....	....
Brewster,	Sears'	Mrs. Susan Sears,	....	....
Bridgewater,	Hyland	Lorenzo D. Monroe	....	....
Brimfield,	Brimfield	Amos Monroe	, ...	....

MASSACHUSETTS.

TOWN.	HOTEL.	PROPRIETOR.			
Brookfield,	Brookfield	J. B. Gass,			
"	Central	W. J. Vizard,	1.50	AF	D ..
W. "	Blair's	L. A. Blair,			
" "	Mossman's	Jerome Mossman,			
N. "	Bartlett's	Mrs. M. Bartlett,			
Brockton,	Brockton	F. B. Washburn,	1.50	AJ	.. ..
"	Montello	F. W. DeCosta,	1.25	AD	D ..
"	Standish	Prince E. Penniman	2.00	AI	.. ..
Cambridge	Cambridge	John G. Lewis,	1.50	AF	H 18
"	Ross'	Maj. H. P. Ross,	2.00	AJ	G ..
Charlemont,	Franklin	D. A. Dalrymple,	1.50	x	.. ..
Chatham,	Eldridge	Mrs. Atkins,			
Chelsea,	Chelsea	J. Linehan,			
"	City	J. Sweeter,	2.00	x	.. ..
Cheshire,	Perkins	F. L. Jenks,			
Chester,	Chester	W. R. White,	2.00	x	.. ..
Chesterfield,	Kelso's	Joseph Kelso,			
Chicopee Falls,	Wildes'	Ansen F. Wildes,	2.00	AH	G ..
Clinton,	Cooke's	J. W. Cook,			
Concord,	Middlesex	Wm. F. Wood & Co.			
Conway,	Conway	Wm. W. Orcutt,			
Cummington,	Grant	Luther C. Eaton,	1.50	AH	D ..
Dalton,	Eagle	J. C. Chamberlain,	2.00	AI	G 15
Danvers,	Danvers	Franklin Howard,	2.00	x	.. ..
Dedham,	Phenix	Mrs. J. D. Howe,	2.00	AH	H ..
"	Union	F. D. Kleinm,			
Deerfield,	Aldrich's	Chas. P. Aldrich,			
"	Pocomptuc	Charles O. Philipps,	2.00	AF	F ..
Dennis,	Cape Cod Bay	J. M. Lufkin,	1.50	AF	F ..
Douglass,	Dudley's	James H. Dudley,	2.00	x	.. ...
Duxbury,	Hollis'	J. B. Hollis,			
East Hampton,	Mansion	William Hill,	2.00	x	.. ...
Edgarton,	Kelley's	Joseph Kelley,			
"	Sea Side	George A. Smith,	2.50	....	15 ..
Fair Haven,	Union	Charles H. Allen,	1.50	AJ	8 ..
Fall River,	Columbian	Alex. Curran,			
"	La Grange	Case & Manchester,	2.50	AL	K ..
"	Thurston's	Vernon Thurston,			
"	Wilbur's	Daris Wilbur,	3.00	AL	K ..
Falmouth,	Baker's	E. E. Hartwell,	1.50	AF	F ..
"	Succanesett	E. E. C. Swift,	2.00	AG	H ..
Fitchburg,	Fitchburg	Joseph Waterhouse	3.00		.... ..
"	Palmer's	Thomas Palmer,			
"	Rollstone	William F. Day,	2.00	AI	G 14

TOWN.	HOTEL.	PROPRIETOR.			
Florence,	Florence	James Stone,	....		
Florida,	Rice's	Jenks & Rice,	....		
Foxboro,	Cocassett	Wm. Adams,	....		
Franklin,	Central	M. H. Johnson,	2.00	AI	I ..
Framingham	S. Framingham,	S. F. Twitchell,	....		
Gardiner,	S. Gardiner	L. H. Horton,	....		
Georgetown,	Poor's	Geo. Poor,	2.00	x	....
Gloucester,	Pavillion	Sherburne & Co.,	....		
Goshen,	Highland	Joseph Hawkes,	2.00	x	....
Grafton,	Farnumsville	Leander White,	....		
Granville,	Granville	Albert Hayden,	2.00	x	....
Great Barrington,	Collins S. R.	Alfred Peck,	2.00	AG	G 17
" "	Pixley's	Mrs. E. Pixley,	....		
Greenfield,	Mansion	George Doolittle,	3.00	AL	....
"	Union	John Fitzgerald,	2.00	AI	10 ..
Greenwich,	Greenwich	T. W. Crombie,	1.50	x	....
Groton,	Central	J. N. Hoar,	2.00	AI	I 18
Grouts Corner,	Grouts Corner	Goodwin&Dudley,	....		
Hadley,	Thayer's	S. H. Thayer,	2.00	x	....
S.Hadley Falls,	Palmers'	Mrs. J. H. Palmer,	....		
Hancock,	White's	M. L. White,	....		
Hardwick,	Hardwick	A. C. Record,	....		
Harvard,	Elm	H. A. Jenkins,	....		
Harwichport,	Sea Side	Judah Chase,	2.00	AI	I ..
Hatfield,	Hatfield	L. S. Bliss,	2.00	AG	G 16
Haverhill,	American	S. R. Batchelder,	....		
"	Elm	A J. Hill,	1.50	AF	....
"	Etna	A. S. Holt,	2.00	AH	H ..
"	Kenoza	John Montgomery,	....		
Haydenville,	Haydenville	Loomis & Son,	1.50	x	....
Hingham,	Cushing	George Cushing 2d,	2.50	AJ	I ..
Hinsdale,	Hinsdale	P. H. Coyle,	1.50	AF	F ..
Holbrook,	Holbrook	D. A. Talbot,	1.50	x	....
Holliston,	Clark's	Willard I. Clark,	2.00	x	....
Holyoke,	Hatfield	C. H. Hatfield,	....		
"	Holyoke	E. M. Belden,	2.50	AL	L ..
HoosacTunnel,	Tower's	A. D. Tower,	2.00	....	10 ..
Hopkinton,	Highland	H. P. Snow,	1.50	AH	E 12
Hubbardstown,	Crystal	J. Fellows,	2.00	AI	E 14
Hudson,	Mansion	Stephen A. Holt,	2.00	x	....
Hull,	Ripley's	N. Ripley & Son,	....		
"	Sargent's	Moses Sargent,	....		
Huntington,	Parks	Joseph Lafleur,	....		

TOWN.	HOTEL.	PROPRIETOR.			
Hyannis,	Iyanough	H. B. Nickerson,	2.00		
Hyde Park,	Everitt	James Patterson,	1.50 AJ	F	
Indian Orchard,	Indian Leap	Samuel Pearce,	2.00 AI	8	
Ipswich,	Smith's	Mrs. Mary D. Smith	1.50 x		
Kingston,	Patuxet	Josiah Cushman,			
Lancaster,	N. Lancaster	Chas. Fairbanks,			
Lanesboro,	American	George Hall,	1.00 AI	7	
"	Lanesboro	Walter P. Corcoran			
Lawrence,	Boston	Banfield & Co.,			
"	Franklin	F. R. Dana,			
Lee,	Jones'	Alfred A Jones,			
"	Morgan	W. C. Winegar,	2.00	10	
"	Norton's	Thomas Norton,	2.00 AH	D	
Lenox,	Curtis'	W. O. Curtis			
Leominster,	Leominster	George H. Cole,			
Lexington,	Hancock	Charles Adair,			
Lowell,	American	Charles Going,			
"	City	Alvin Emerson,	2.00 AJ	J	
"	Franklin	C. C. Copeland,			
"	Globe	John Cusack,	1.50 AD	D	
"	Harris'	Frank H. Harris,			
"	Howard	Ebenezar Morgan,			
"	Merrimac	Emery & Nute,	2.50	14	
"	Middlesex	Almond Wood,			
"	Tremont	J. H. Durgin, Jr.,			
"	Washington	Frank E. Shaw,			
Lynn,	Kirtland	H. S. Bowles,			
"	Sagamore	W. C. Thompson,			
Magnolia,	Crescent Beach	Allen Knowlton,	3.00 AN	20	
Malden,	Evelyn	Joseph Sweetser,	2.50 AK	H	
"	Pratt's	John Pratt,			
Manchester,	Manchester	Josiah Peabody,	2.00 x		
Mansfield,	Mansfield	Thomas R. Trippe,	2'00 AI	8	14
Marblehead,	Dennis'	John C. Dennis,			
"	Ware's	Benj. P. Ware,			
Marion,	Bay View	J. S. Luce,	2.00 AJ	J	
Marlborough,	Central	Hatch & Leighton,	1.50	8	
"	Marlboro	W. H. Leighton Jr.,	1.50 AH	F	16
Marshfield,	Churchill's	George Churchill,	2.00 AJ	J	
"	Webster	L. J. MaDan,	2.00 AJ	I	17
Mattapoisett,	Mattapoisett	Wm. H. Stimson,			
Medford,	Emerson's	A. J. Emerson,			
Medway,	Pike's	A. J. Pike,			
Mendon,	Mendon	W. Coleman,	1.50 AF	F	15

TOWN.	HOTEL.	PROPRIETOR.				
Methuen,	Exchange	S. Q. Hersey,	2.00	AI	I	..
Middleboro,	Cushman's	A. H. Cushman,				
"	Methuen	John R. Jones,				
Milford,	Fisher's	Lewis Fisher,				
"	Milford	S. E. Hapgood,	2.00	AI	I	18
Millbury,	**St. Charles**	Charles T. Pratt,	1.50	AF	F	18
Millers Falls,	Goodnow's	Samuel Goodnow,				
Mill River,	Mill River	Harbron Rogers,				
Monroe,	Goodell's	David Goodell,				
Montague,	Wilde's	Samuel C. Wildes,	2.50	x		..
Monterey,	Tyron's	Albert Tyron,				
Nahant,	Hood Cottage S. R.,	F. A. Goell,	3.50	AP	O	..
"	Moore's	Nathan Moore,				
Nantucket,	Mowrey's	A. S. Mowrey,				
"	Sherburne	John W. Macy,	2.50		15	..
Natick,	Sherman's	C. H. Sherman,				
South Natick,	Bailey's	G. Bailey & Son,				
New Bedford,	Avon	Otis Parlow,	1.50	x		..
"	German	Leopold Bartel,	1.00	x		..
"	Mansion	Lewis Boutell,	2.00	x		..
"	Mariners	H. G. O'Nye,	1.00	x		..
"	Mt. Pleasant	Edward Wing,	2.00	x		..
"	Parkers	N. M. Brownell,	3.00	x		..
"	Whitcomb	E. R. Richards,	1.50	x		..
New Boston,	Hunt's	C. H. Hunt,				
Newburyport,	American	Daniel Hamblett,	2.00	AH	G	..
"	**Merrimac**	J. A. Shattuck,	2.50	AJ	J	20
"	Noyes'	S.B. & J.H.Noyes,				
"	Ocean	J. P. L. Westcott,	2.00	AI	I	18
"	Wentworth's	Wm.B.Wentworth				
New Marlboro,	Centre	Ira N. Tuttle,				
North Salem	North Salem	Moses Herrick,				
Newtown,	Cate's	Stephen Cate,				
Northampton,	Prospect	John W. French,	2.50	AL	14	..
"	Round Hill	Irad Fuller,	3.00	AL	K	..
"	Smith's	Edwin R. Smith,				
Northfield,	Northfield	James S. Pickard,				
Norton,	Mansion	John H. Short,				
Orange,	Putnam's	A. P. Putnam,	2.00	AI	J	..
Orleans,	Higgins	James Chandler,	1.50	AI	7	..
Otis,	Day's	Edward D. Day,				
East Otis	East Otis	D. Norris,				
Oxford,	Sibley's	B. F. Sibley,				

MASSACHUSETTS.

TOWN.	HOTEL.	PROPRIETOR.			
Palmer,	American	J. S. Wood,	2.00	AI	11 ..
"	Weeks'	J. W. Weeks,	....	....	.. ..
Paxton,	Summit,	Wm. W. Dodd,	....	....	.. ..
Peabody,	Naumkeag,	H. W. Moore,	....,	....	.. ..
"	Simonds'	Wash'n Simonds,	....	....	.. ..
E. Pepperell,	Williams'	Luther F. Williams,	....	....	.. ..
Pigeon Cove,	Pigeon Cove	Mrs. E. Robinson,	....	....	.. ..
Pittsfield,	American	C. Quackenbush,	....	....	.. ..
"	Berkshire	Reilly Denning,	....	....	.. ..
"	Burbank	Abraham Burbank	....	....	.. ..
Plymouth,	Central	Chas. H. Snell,	1.50	AF	F ..
"	Old Colony	N. M. Perry,	2.00	AI	I ..
"	Samoset S. R.	P. C. Chandler,	2.50	AJ	12 ...
"	Standish	P. E. Benjamin,	2.00	AH	.. ..
Princeton,	Beaman's	P. A. Beaman & Son,	....	....	.. ..
"	Prospect S. R.	George L. Bliss,	2.00	AI	I ..
Provincetown,	Central	Allen Reed,	2.00	AJ	.. ..
"	Smith's	Frank Smith,	....	....	.. ..
Quincy,	Great Hill	James Mears,	2.00	AJ	10 ..
"	Willow	G. L. Odiorne,	....	....	.. ..
Randolph,	Hathaway's	Wm.B.Hathaway,	....	....	.. ..
Revere,	Cove	George Wilkinson,	....	....	.. ..
"	Tapley's	Geo. A. Tapley,	....	....	.. ..
"	Tarlton's	Tarlton & West,	....	....	.. ..
Rochdale,	Camwell's	James Camwell,	....	....	.. ..
S. Royalston,	Moore's	Richard Moore,	2.00	x	.. ..
Russell,	Russell	Louis Herrick,	....	....	.. ..
Salem,	Essex	Palmer & Farnsworth,	3.00	x	.. ..
"	Salem	Edwin A. Southwick,	1.25	A H	7 ..
East Salisbury,	Atlantic	J.F.& E.J.Morrill,	3.00	AN	L ..
Sandwich,	Chadwick's	Z. F. Chadwick,	....	....	.. ..
Savory,	Green Mountain	Calvin Bowker,	....	....	.. ..
Scituate,	Torrey's	W. S. Torrey,	....	....	.. ..
Sharon,	Massapoag S. R.	Thos. Decatur & Bro..	3.00	AM	N ..
Sheffield,	Miller's	S. R. Miller,	2.00	AI	I ..
Shelburne Falls,	Shelburne Falls	Cole & Lampman,	2.00	AI	I 18
Somerville,	American	John W. Whiting,	....	....	.. ..
"	Elm	John Alexander,	....	....	.. ..
Southampton,	Swan's	MrsAnnieM.Swan	2.00	x	...
Southbridge,	Parker's	J. F. Parker,,	2.00	x	...

MASSACHUSETTS.

TOWN.	HOTEL.	PROPRIETOR.	
Southwick,	Union	S. M. Hunt,	....
Spencer,	Spencer	Ira E. Lackey,	....
Springfield.			
....	Bates'	F. G. Bates,	....
....	Berkshire	Edward L. Allen,	1.50 AF E ..
....	Carlton	A. Hanrahan,	....
....	Cooley's	J. M. Cooley,	....
....	Exchange	E. Adams & Co.,	2.00 AJ I ..
....	Guendlers	Berthold Winkler,	....
....	Haynes'	Tilly Haynes,	....
....	Marshall	William M. Bemis,	2.00 AI I ..
....	Massasoit	M. & E. S. Chapin,	....
....	Nayassett	Wm. L. Clegg,	....
....	Pynchon	Wetherbee & Neal	....
....	Union	F. E. French,	....
State Line,	State Line	James P. Murphy,	....
Stockbridge,	Stockbridge	Mrs.M.H.Plumb,	....
West "	Sweet's	Norris L. Sweet,	....
Stoneham,	Melvin's	Charles B. Melvin,	....
Stoughton,	Drake's	Leonard Drake,	....
Stowe,	Minnehaha	Fred. Boyd,	1.25 AD D ..
Swampscott,	Wardwell's	S. H. Wardwell,	....
Swansea,	Case's	Joseph Case,	....
Taunton,	City	A. L. Bliss,	3.00 AL L ..
"	"	"	1.00 EG .. ..
"	Central	G. C. Kelley,	2.00 A 9 ..
"	Exchange	L. E. Francis,	1.25 AD D ..
"	Everitt	C. A. Oakes,	....
"	St. Cloud	W. H. Harlow,	....
".	Washington	M. H. Davis,	....
Templeton,	Otter River	J. W. Partridge,	....
Topsfield,	Topsfield	A. M. Munday,	....
Townsend Centre,	Terrell's	John E. Terrell,	....
Turners Falls,	Farren	G. T. C. Holden	....
Vineyard Haven,	Mansion	Samuel Look,	....
Waltham,	Prospect	Gideon Haynes,	....
Ware,	Hampshire	Reuben Snow,	2.00 AI I 14
"	Ware	Thomas Kendrick,	....
Wareham,	Hackett's	P. G. Hackett,	....
Watertown,	Nesmith's	J. J. Nesmith,	....
Wayland,	Simpson's	T. H. Simpson,	....

MASSACHUSETTS.

TOWN.	HOTEL.	PROPRIETOR.		
Webster,	Fuller	C. W. Fuller,	2.00 A H G	16
"	**Joslin's**	Horace I. Joslin,	2.50 A I H	..
Wellfleet,	Holbrook's	Mrs. S. Holbrook,	....	..
Westboro,	Westboro	Dollin K. Sherman	2.00 A J	....
Westfield,	Buschman's	John Buschman,	....	..
"	Foster's	Mrs. S. N. Foster,	....	..
Westminster,	Westminster	Samuel B. Beaman,	....	..
Wilbraham,	Allis'	Mrs. M. E. Allis & Son,	2.00 A F	6 10
Williamstown,	Mansion	A. G. Bailey,	3.00 A L K	..
South "	S. Williamstown	Nathan Field,	....	..
Winchenden,	American	Wm. Lumflin,	2.00 A I	6 ..
Woburn,	Central	S. A. Hartshorn,	....	..
Worcester.				
283 Main St.,	Bay State	H. Barnes & Co.,	....	..
....	Elmwood	D. J. Baker,	....	..
93 Main,	Exchange	W. F. Weeks,	2.00	10 ..
648 Main,	Grand Central	T. Jameson,	....	..
....	Lincoln	S. W. Balcom,	....	..
....	New Brewster	Thomas Kendrick,	1.50 A H	6 ..
Belmont,	Quinsigamond	Clifford & Tower,	....	..
25 Waldo,	Waldo	R. W. & L. B. Stuart,	....	..
Worthington,	Bartlett's	Jacob M. Bartlett,	....	..
"	Worthington	....	1.25 A F	7 ..

RHODE ISLAND.

Apponaug,	Apponaug	Jas. H. Atwood,	2.00 A I	10 ..
Bristol,	Bristol	M. V. Newton,	....	..
Chepachet,	**Eddy's**	J. M. Eddy,	2.00 A I	I ..
Crompton,	Booth's	Wright Booth,	....	..
Cumberland,	Cook's	Edmund L. Cook,	....	..
EastGreenwich	Kent	R. G. Brown,	....	..
" "	Updike's	Misses A & A Updike	....	..
Hopkinton,	Hope Valley	F. M. Burton,	....	..
Kingston,	Kingston	J. S. Brown,	2.00 A I	....
Naragansett Pier	Atlantic	Abijah Browning	3.50 A O	O ..
"	" Delavan	J. G. Burns,	3.00 A N	18 ..
"	" Mettatoxett	John H. Caswell	2.50	15 ..
Newport,	Aquidneck SR	Philip Rider	....	..
"	Howard St.	John France	....	..
"	Ocean S. R.	Weaver & Bates,	....	..
"	Pelham St.	James T. Potter,	....	..
"	United States	Walter Corbett,	....	..

TOWN.	HOTEL.	PROPRIETOR.			
New Shoreham	Ocean View	Nicholas Ball,	3.50	A M	N ..
Olneyville,	Matteson's	John Matteson,		......	
Pawtucket,	Benedict	J. E. Ross,	2.50	A L	.. ..
"	Pawtucket	P. E. Penniman		......	
Pawtuxet,	Kearsage	Daniel Howard,		......	
Phenix,	Phenix	Andrew Rhodes,	2.00	A H	9 ..
Providence.					
46 Union St.	**Adams**	Samuel H. Wales, Jr.	2.00	A J	J 21
92 N. Main	American	John C. Payne,	2.00	....	9 ..
6 Canal	Central	Hopkins & Sears,	1.50	E J	.. ..
150 Broad	City	L. H. Humphreys,	4.00	......	
49 Chestnut	Chestnut	Mrs. Tanner,		......	
118 N. Main	Clarendon	J. H. Higgins,	1.50	x	.. ..
421 High	Hopkins	Frank Whipple,	1.50	A F	F ..
N. Main & N. Court	Providence	John Sweeny,	2.00	x	.. ..
261 Westminster	Westminster	F. W. Huntoon,	2.50	A L	L 25
Scituate,	Scranton's	A. J. Scranton,		......	
South Scituate,	Miller	F. M. Miller,	1.50	....	5 ..
Smithfield,	Greenville	John F. Crump,		......	
Tiverton,	Lawton's	George Lawton,		......	
Warren,	Niles'	Wm. B. Niles,		......	
Warwick,	Apponaug	Jas. H. Atwood,	2.00	A I	10 ..
"	Warwick	Amos Wells,	2.50	......	
Watch Hill,	Plimpton's	A. S. Plimpton,	3.50	A M	.. ..
" "	Sea Side	D. F. Larkin & Co.,	4.00	A R	R ..
Westerly,	Leonard	T. A. Carpenter,	2.00	A I	9 ..
"	Spencer's	O. S. Spencer		......	
Wickford,	Washington	Anson Matteson,	2.00	A I	9 ..
Woonsocket,	Monument	L. W. Elliot,		......	
"	Woonsocket,	Cook, Mason & Co.,		......	
Wyoming,	Dawley	Amos J. Dawley,		......	

CONNECTICUT.

TOWN.	HOTEL.	PROPRIETOR.			
Andover,	Dorrance's	Wm. Dorrance,			
Ansonia,	Elmore's	E. S. Elmore,			
"	Rail Road	James Dermay,	1.50		8 ..
Ashford,	Clarke's	Dyer H. Clarke,			
Baltic,	Baltic	R. J. Brophy,	2.00	AI	8 14
Berlin,	Berlin	Henry A. Gwatkins			
Birmingham,	Bassett	Charles T. Wells,	3.00		
Bolton,	Bolton	William H. Hunt,	2.00	AF	7 14
Branford,	Indian Neck	Eli Goodrich,	2.00	AF	F 18
"	Lounsbury's	David Lounsbury,			
"	Way's	James R. Way,			
Bridgeport,	American	Geo. G. Thompson,			
"	Atlantic	A. R. Lamb,			
"	Sterling	Atwood & Whiting,			
Bristol,	Bristol	Pierce & Norton,			
"	Central	Mrs. P. Schwarzweller,	1.50		7 ..
"	Commercial	L. P. Goodwin,	2.00	A H G	17
Brookfield,	Brookfield	John Kane,	1.50	AF	6 12
Brooklyn,	Brooklyn	Charles C. Burdick,	2.00	AI	I ..
Canaan,	Riker's	D. A. Riker,			
Canton,	Hawks'	A. P. Hawks,			
Central Village,	Collins'	John D. Collins, Jr.			
Chester,	Weaver's	Erastus Weaver,			
Clinton,	Smith's	Richard P. Smith,			
Colchester,	Gabrielle's	Chas. Gabrielle,			
W. Cornwall,	Mansion	Anthony Miller,			
Coventry,	Loomis'	S. T. Loomis,	1.25	AC	6 ..
Danbury,	Pahquioque	Platt S. Osborn,	2.00	AJ	I ..
"	Turners	S. E. Hapgood,			
"	Wooster	O. E. Austin,	2.50		
Dayville,	Dayville	L. M. Kennedy,	2.00	AI	F ..
Deep River,	**Wahginnicut**	William D. Worthington,	2.00	AI	I 18
Derby,	Birmingham	....	2.00	AI	G ..
"	**Union**	George L. Thomas,	2.00	AH	F ..
Enfield	Hazardville	S. Charter,			
East Hampton,	Pokatapang	Wm. G. Buell,	1.50		10 ..
East Haven,	Nettleton's	Geo. D. Nettleton,			
Essex,	'Harrington's	Geo. Harrington,			
"	Welch's	John Welch,			
Fairfield,	Fairfield	Valentine & Willett	2.00	AI	I ..
Falls Village,	Dudley's	E. I. Dudley,	2.00	AI	I ..
"	Peck's	Geo. K. Peck,			

CONNECTICUT. 33

TOWN.	HOTEL.	PROPRIETOR.	
Farmington,	Whitman's	Wm. Whitman,	....
Gildersleeves Landing,	Union	D. B. Williams,	2.00 .... 10 ..
Glasstonbury,	Gaines'	W. H. Gaines,	....
Goshen,	Goshen	C. J. Soudant,	....
Granby,	Benjamin's	Samuel Benjamin,	....
"	Hayden's	E. Hayden,	....
East Granby,	Union	Frank Granger,	....
Greenville,	Greenville	T. Cunningham,	2.00 AI I ..
Greenwich,	Half Way	S. W. Newman,	....
"	Lenox S. R.	A. J. Rutges,	....
Guilford,	**Guilford**	E. M. Sherman,	2.00 .... 10 ..
"	Hunt's	James A. Hunt,	....
Haddam,	Champion	D. Watrous,	2.00 AI G ..
Hartford.			
High&AllenSt.	Adams'	G. F. Adams,	2.00 AJ G ..
Asylum & Trumbull,	Allyn	T.M.& R.J.Allyn,	....
....	Bacon	Redfield,	....
217 Main,	**City**	N. W. Taylor,	3.00 .... 18 ..
28 Market,	Derby's	Augustus Derby,	2.00 .... 11 ..
High cor.Allyn	**Park Central**	E. G. Hastings,	4.00 AN O ..
554 Main,	Sigourney	N. J. Coyle,	2.00 AJ I ..
6FarmingtonAv.	Union Hall	A. J. Pease & Co.,	2.00 AI I ..
26 State,	United States	D. A. Rood,	3.00 AM.... ..
Hazardville,	Charter's	Sylvester Charter,	....
Hebron,	American	Horace F. Porter,	1.50 AF 6 ..
Jewett City,	Jewett City	Ira F. Lewis,	....
Kent,	Comstock's	DanielB.Comstock	....
Killingly,	Attawaugan	Lewis Worden,	....
"	Danielsonville	Chas.E. Hutchins,	1.50 AH 6 ..
"	Olive Branch	Clark B. Cornell,	1.50 AH D ..
Lakeville,	Miller's	Miller Bros.	....
Litchfield,	Crossman's	Wm. H. Crossman,	....
Lyme,	Lyme	E. E. Clark,	1.50 AH 7 ..
Manchester,	Knox's	C. B. Knox,	2.00 AH G ..
Meriden,	Bixbee's	Theodore Bixbee,	.75 EE ....
"	Mechanics'	M. Moran,	....
W. "	Brentnal's	P. L. Brentnal,	....
" "	Meriden	A. H. Bradley,	3.00 .... 10 ..
" "	Curtis	Mrs. J. Taylor,	....
Middletown,	Air Line	Thomas Furniss,	1.50 AH 8 ..
"	Farmers & Mechanics	C. N. Brainard,	....

2

TOWN.	HOTEL.	PROPRIETOR.	
Middletown,	McDonough	J. S. Dickinson,	3.00 AL L ..
"	New York	Donahue & Bro.,	....
Milford,	Sparks'	N. J. Sparks & Co.	....
Moosup,	Kenyon	D. K. Douglass,	....
"	Young's	Horace P. Young,	....
Mystic Bridge,	Hoxie's	B. F. Hoxie,	....
Naugatuck,	Naugatuck	George D. Squires,	2.00 AI J ..
New Britain,	Bassett's	C. Bassett,	....
"	New Britain	John A. Tryon,	....
"	Union	John Howson,	1.00 AA A ..
New Canaan,	Taylor's	Leroy Taylor,	....
New Haven.			
State cor. George, St. Union cor.	Austin,	Orson Austin & Sons,	2.50 AN .. ..
Wooster,	City	James Barker,	2.00 AI I ..
153 Chapel,	Elliott	R. Dyer,	....
73 Union,	Florence,	C. W. Bradley,	....
264 State,	Madison	Wm. Doolittle,	2.25 AK K ..
444 Chapel,	New Haven	S. H. Mosely,	....
51 Court,	Thomas'	Alfred Thomas,	1.50 AE E ..
.. Church,	Tontine	J. W. Bradley,	....
New London.			
....	Atlantic,	Theodore John	2.00 AI J ..
....	Metropolitan	R. P. Freeman,	....
....	National	Ticknor & Hutchinson,	2.00 AJ .. ..
....	Steamboat	Wm. & J.L.Bacon,	....
....	Pequod S. R.	H. S. Crocker,	....
New Milford,	Bristol's	Isaac B. Bristol,	....
Niantic,	Howard	Chas. Babcock,	....
Newtown,	Central	Douglass Fairchild	2.00 AJ 10 ..
Norfolk,	Dick's	Wm. J. Dick,	....
"	Norfolk	G. B. Jaycox,	2.25 AJ .. ..
Norwalk,	Connecticut	Mrs. J. Burke,	....
"	Taylor's	L. Taylor,	2.50 AJ .. ..
SouthNorwalk,	City	H. H. Bartlett,	2.50 AK K ..
"	French's	C. G. French,	2.50 AI I ..
"	Stedman's	F. F. Stedman & Sons,	....
Norwich,	American	A. L. Clark,	2.50 AI I 18
"	Chelsea	Edwin Fay,	1.00 EG .. ..
"	Thames	J. W. Sorell,	....

TOWN.	HOTEL.	PROPRIETOR.		
Norwich,	Uncas	T. A. Holmes,	1.50	
"	United States	F. Richter,		
"	Wauregan	C. W. Johnson,	3.00	
Oxford,	Oxford	E. L. Warner,		
Plainfield,	Austin's	C. W. Austin,		
"	Plainfield	Fowler & Clark,	2.00	A H 6
Plainville,	Tinker's	Frank A. Tinker,		
Plymouth,	Quiet	A. B. Curtis,		
Poquonock,	Village	Gaylord Hitchcock	1.25	A D C
Putnam,	Elm St.	W. B. White,		
"	Quinebaug	D. Casewell,		
Rainbow,	Rainbow	Dana L. Payne,		
Rockville,	Reeney's	E. & F. Reeney,		
Rocky Hill,	Shipman's	Samuel Shipman,		
Salisbury,	Russell's	Theodore Russell,		
Sandy Hook,	Sandy Hook	Edward Taylor,		
New Saybrook,	Fenwick Hall	D. A. Rood,		
Seymour,	Merwin's	Sidney Merwin,		
"	Dunham's	A. B. Dunham,		
Sharon,	Sharon	Mrs. S. L. Potter,		
Somers,	United States	Warren Kibbe		
Southington,	Bradley	S. C. Hooker,	2.00	A I 1
Stafford,	Plimpton's	Paley Plimpton,		
Stamford,	Hamilton S. R.	S. T. Cozzens,		
"	Kingman's	F. Kingman,		
"	Union	B. F. Wallace,		
"	Williams'	A. W. Williams,	1.50	A F F
Stonington,	Tremont	Richard R. Barker,		
Suffield,	Knox'	Knox Brothers,	1.50	A H E
Tareffville,	Reed's	Wm. Reed,		
"	Thurston's	A. L. F. Thurston,		
Thompson,	Thompson	Stephen Crosby,		
Thompsonville,	Thompsonville	B. F. Lord,		
Tolland,	County,		2.00	A J J
"	Olmstead's	Geo. H. Olmstead,		
Unionville,	Dunham's	Chas. Dunham,		
Voluntown,	Union	Hiram Jenks,		
Wallingford,	Hoey's	Lawrence Hoey,		
Washington,	Ford's	R. W. Ford,		
Waterbury,	Meyers	John Pfaff,		
"	Scovill	J. Doolittle,	3.00	A L 20
"	**Waterbury**	E. H. Hayes,	2.50	10
Waterford,	Sandy Point	John H. Manwaring,	2.00	A I 1

TOWN.	HOTEL.	PROPRIETOR.			
Watertown,	Warren	Mrs. O. B. King,	....	....	..
Waterville	Waterville	Lawrence Ruth,	....	....	..
Westbrook,	Westbrook	Geo. C. Moore,	....	....	..
West Haven,	Hinman's	Preston H. Hinman	....	....	..
"	Sea View	George R. Kelsey,	....	....	..
Westport,	Westport	David S. Gray,	....	....	..
Willimantic	Brainerd	D. Lathrop,	2.00	A I	I ..
"	National	A. A. Snow,	2.00	A I	I ..
Windsor,	Alford	E. S. Alford,	....	....	..
Windsor Locks,	**Charter Oak**	Henry Cutler,	2.00	A I	7 ..
Winsted,	Clarke	E. Y. Morehouse,	2.00	A I	I ..
"	Forrester's	John R. Forrester,	....	....	..
West Winsted,	Beardsley	E. C. Stevens,	2.00	A I	I ..
Wolcottville,	Allen's	Henry J. Allen,	2.50	A I	I ..
"	Wells'	H. Wells,	....	....	..
Woodbury,	McMartry's	Mrs. McMartry,	....	....	..
"	Travers'	James W. Travers,	....	....	..
Woodstock,	Elmwood Hall	....	1.50	A E	E ..
South "	Stear's	A. L. Stear,	....	....	..

NEW YORK. 37

TOWN.	HOTEL.	PROPRIETOR.		
Adams,	Huson's	Arthur B. Huson,		
Addison,	Brant's	A. L. Brant,		
"	Exchange	James E. Smith,		
Afton,	Musson's	Richard Musson,		
Akron,	American	F. Fink,	2.00 A E F	..
Alabama,	Clark	Charles Clark,	2.00 AJ	5 ..
Albany.				
274 Broadway,	Burns'	J. F. Burns,		
719 "	City	John A. Gladding,		
Broadway cor. Steuben St.,	Delavan	Chas. E. Leland & Co.,		
100 State Church cor.	Eldredge's	Eldredge & Son,		
John,	Empire	P. Murphy,	2.00	14 ..
7 S. Pearl,	Globe	Jas. A. Honck,		
34 Beaver,	Germania	John Bissikimmer,		
387 Broadway,	Mansion	Wm. Thompson,	2.00 AJ	1 ..
Broadway & Maiden Lane,	Messenger	E. J. Kearney,	0.75 EE	.. ..
Broadway & Madison Av.,	Oneonta	Martin Fryer,	1.50 AD	6 ..
170 S. Pearl,	Pearl St.	W. Edward Stiles,	2.00	11 ..
Broadway & Maiden Lane,	Stanwix Hall	Delavan Peck,		
Albion,	Mansion	B. Ball,		
"	Orleans	Taylor & Son,	2.00	
"	Warner's	Marvin Warner,		
Alden,	Patterson's	G. F. Patterson,	1.25 AD C	..
Alder Creek,	Thurston's	Geo. L. Thurston,		
Alexander,	Heintz's	John Heintz,		
AlexandriaBay	Crossman	C.Crossman & Son	2.50	.. ..
Alfred,	Alfred	Clark L. Wilter,		
Alleghany,	Ward's	D. Ward,	2.00 AF	8 14
Alma,	Forest	C. G. Watkins,	1.50 AD	C 11
Almond,	Green's	B. F. Green & Co.		
Altoona,	Travellers Home	John McGregor,	1.50 AD	5 10
Amenia,	Pratt's	Peter Pratt,	2.00 x	.. ..
"	Tuttle	Chas. H. Tuttle,		
Amityville,	South Side	Mrs. E. C. King & Son,		
Amsterdam,	Amsterdam	Schuyler DeForest	2.00 x	.. ..
"	Fox	James Fox,	1.50 x	.. ..
"	McDonnell	J. W. Ingalls,	2.00 x	.. ..
"	Tremont	Frederick Deal,	2.00	7 ..

TOWN.	HOTEL.	PROPRIETOR.			
Andes,	Central	Pratt Chamberlin,	2.00	AE	7 ..
Angelica,	Charles	Joseph Gillies,	2.00	AG G	15
Antwerp,	Foster's	T. M. Foster,	2.00	AG	8 ..
Arcade,	Calkins'	Levi Calkins,	....	......	..
Argyle,	Shannon's	White & Shannon,	2.00	....	12 ..
Ashland,	Ashland Centre	David Traver,	1.50	AD	8 15
Athens,	Robbins'	Joseph Robbins,	2.00	AH	7 ..
"	Wormer's	John C. Wormer,	2.00	AI	....
Attica,	Exchange	S. L. Austin,	2.00	AH	6 10
"	St. James	John Wolfe,	1.50	x	....
"	Washburn's	J. B. Washburn,	2.00	AE A	..
"	Western	Wm. E. Blakeley,	2.00	x	....
Auburn,	Exchange	M. P. Morgan,	2.00	AH	....
"	Louis	Louis Schuch,	2.00	x	....
"	National	C. B. Delano,	2.00	x	....
"	Osborne	B. Ashby,	3.50	AN	....
"	St. James	S. P. Chapman,	3.00	AL	....
"	Tremont	M. P. Morgan,	2.00	x	....
Augusta,	Knoxboro	G. W. Brigham,	....	......	..
Auriesville,	Aurelins	D. C. Faulkner,	....	......	..
Ausable Forks,	American	John Hargraves,	2.00	AF	F 16
"	Ausable	Chas. H. Kendall,	2.00	AG	G 17
Ava,	Egger's	Frank Egger,	....	......	..
Avon,	Congress Hall	O. D. Phelps,	2.50	....	16 ..
"	Knickerbocker	J. E. Smedley,	2.00	x	....
"	National	Wm. E. Pattee,	2.00	x	....
East Avon,	Newman's	Isaac R. Newman	1.50	AF	F ..
Babylon,	American	Mrs. P. A. Seaman	....	......	..
"	Sumpwams	Charles T. Duryea	....	......	..
"	Washington	John Lux,	2.00	AI	I ..
"	Watson	Selah C. Smith,	....	......	..
Bainbridge,	Hastings'	W. M. & W. W. Hastings,	....	......	..
Bakers Bridge,	Alfred	Clark L. Witter,	1.00	AB	A ..
Baldwinsville,	Seneca	Len Faucher,	2.00	AI	7 ..
Ballston Spa,	Ballston Spa	George Smith,	2.00	....	10 ..
"	Marsden's	James E. Marsden	2.00	AH	J ..
"	Medbury's	S. B. Medbury,	2.00	....	10 ..
"	San Souci	William Stott,	3.00	x	....
Barryville,	Atkins'	J. H. Atkins, Jr.,	1.25	AC	5 10
"	Riverview	W. W. Cortright,	1.50	AF	F ..
Batavia,	St. James	A. G. Collins & Co.	3.00	......	..
"	Washburn's	John Washburn & Son,	2.00	....	11 ..

NEW YORK.

TOWN.	HOTEL.	PROPRIETOR.			
Bath,	Gilmore	H. E. Jones,	2.00	AF	E 12
"	Mansion	Perry Topping.	1.50	x	.. ..
"	Nichols	J. R. Laidlaw,	2.00	AI	I ..
"	Stenben	D.H.Wright&Son	1.50	x	.. ..
Bay Shore,	Dominy's	Mrs. F. Dominy,	....	....	.. ..
Beekmantown,	Union	Benj. Simonds,	1.25	AD	C ..
Bellport,	Bellport Bay	Homan & Ritch,	2.50	....	15 ..
Belvidere,	Belvidere,	E. P. Sandborn,	1.50	AD	C ..
"	Western	George M. Fox,	2.00	AI	8 ..
Belmont,	Rail Road	S. C. Phelps,	1.50	AE	E ..
Berlin,	Niles'	A. B. Niles,	....	....	.. ..
Binghampton,	Arbor	Skillman&LaRose	2.00	x	.. ..
"	Cafferty's	C. M. Cafferty,	2.50	x	.. ..
"	Chenango	Charles Wales,	1.50	x	.. ..
"	Dwight	Col.WalterDwight	4.50	x	.. ..
"	Edwards'	R. O. Edwards,	1.75	x	.. ..
"	Exchange	J. G. Devoe,	2.50	x	.. ..
"	Franklin	P. Cahill,	1.75	x	.. ..
"	Lewis	Wm. Shanley,	2.50	x	.. ..
"	Lewis Place	Cyrus Lewis,	2.00	x	.. ..
"	Rogers'	I. Rogers,	1.50	AE	B ..
"	Spaulding's	W. F. Spaulding,	3.00	AL	.. ..
Booneville,	American	Joseph Winkler,	1.50	AD	C ..
"	Hulbert	George A. May,	2.00	x	.. ..
Bradford,	Bradford	John L. Ward,	1.50	....	5 ..
BrashearFalls,	Aldrich's	A. Aldrich,	1.50	AF	F 15
Brewerton,	Washburn's	C. E. Washburn,	2.00	AH	H ..
Bridgehampton	Atlantic	John W. Hull,	2.00	AH	F ..
Bridgewater,	Hibbard's	O. C. Hibbard,	1.50	AE	5 8
Brookfield,	Parks'	W. S. Parks,	2.00	....	5 ..
Brockport,	Central	S. W. Smith,	2.00	AG	G 16
"	Getty's	J. A. Getty,	2.00	A	10 ..
"	Peck's	F. W. Peck,	2.00	....	6 ..
Brooklyn.					
147 Hicks St.,	Mansion	Edwin R. Yale,	3.00	x	.. ..
12 Fulton,	Montauk	J. M. Freeman,	2.00	AI	12 ..
90 Montague,	Pierrepont	Charles N. Peed,	4.00	AP	N ..
Brownville,	Brownville	Bailey & Eaton,	2.00	AG	7 14
"	Johnston's	John Johnston,	1.50	AE	6 ..
Buffalo.					
10 W.Eagle St.,	Bloomer's	T. T. Bloomer,	....	....	.. ..
Seneca cor. Morgan,	Browns	J. Littlefield,	2.00	AI	I ..
Exchange cor. Michigan,	City	P. Hoenig.	2.00	....	.. ..

	HOTEL.	PROPRIETOR.			
Buffalo.					
1518 Main,	Horter's	Wm. Lockwood,	2.00 AI	I	..
Main & Exchange, N. Y. C. R. R.	Mansion,	Andrews & Whitney,	....	....	..
Depot,	National	Jones & Crandall,	....	....	..
1919 Niagara,	North Buffalo	Albert Parmelee,	2.00 AF	8	16
Terrace cor. Main,	United States	D. Bonney & Son,	2.00 AI	J	20
Butternuts,	Peabody's	E. A. Peabody,	....	....	..
Byron,	Byron Centre	Charles Leonard,	1.50 AF	5	..
Cairo,	Walter's	A. L. & F. G. Walters,	....	....	..
Caldwell,	Central	B. O. Brown,	2.00	 10	..
"	Fort George	Seelye & Wood,	3.50	 20	..
Caledonia,	Foote's	P. P. Foote,	....	....	..
Callicoon,	Minard's	B. Minard,	1.50	 6	..
Cambridge,	Central	H. S. Lee,	2.00	 10	..
"	Irving	S. I. Stroud,	2.00 AI	I	..
Camden,	Durr's	Patrick Durr,	....	....	..
"	Whitney's	Moses L. Whitney	....	....	..
Canajoharie,	Eldridge	Chas. H. Lovett,	....	....	..
"	Nellis'	A. Nellis & Co.,	2.00 AI	I	..
Canandaigua,	Canandaigua	Cook & Wakeman,	3.00 AI	14	..
"	Masseth	J. & E. Masseth,	2.00 AI	11	..
"	Washington	W. L. Stetson,	....	....	..
Canastota,	Hale's	Chauncey H. Hale	....	....	..
"	Twogood's	D. C. Twogood,	2.00	 7	..
Canaseraga,	Bennett	H. N. Crandall,	1.50 AH	5	..
Candor,	Murray's	Wm. Murray,	....	....	..
Caneadea,	Oramel	Samuel B. Talman,	....	....	..
Canisteo,	Bennett's	W. W. Bennett,	....	....	..
Canton,	Hodskins	M. F. Spencer,	2.50	 14	..
"	Wood's	D. Wood & Son,	....	....	..
Carthage,	Peck's	M. A. Peck,	....	....	..
Catskill,	Grant	Grant & Cornell,	3.00 x	....	..
"	Greene Co.	Philip C. Gay,	2.00 x	....	..
"	Gunn's	Enos Gunn,	2.00 x	....	..
"	**Irving**	H. A. Person,	3.00 AM	....	..
"	Laurel	J. L. Schutt,	3.00	 15	..
"	Mountain	Chas. L. Beach,	4.50 x	....	..
"	Western	Martin F. Smith,	1.50 AD	D	12
Cattaraugus,	Temperance	D. S. Brown,	....	....	..
Cayuga,	Cayuga Lake	James A. Bailey,	2.00	 10	..
Cazenovia,	Cazenovia	Edmond Jewett,	1.50 AF	5	..

NEW YORK.

TOWN.	HOTEL.	PROPRIETOR.			
Centreville,	Merwin	Nelson Merwin,	1.00	A B	A ..
Champlain,	Champlain	T. P. Field,	2.00	A I	G ..
Charlotte,	Spencer	John Burns,	3.00	A L	L
"	Steamboat	Cornelius O. Cannon	2.00	A I	6 ..
Chatham Village,	Park	F. I. Childs,	1.50	....	6 ..
" "	Stanwix Hall	Miles S. Beach,	2.00	A I	I ..
Chateaugay,	Roberts	T. B. Ladd,	1.50	A H	F 14
" Lake	Lower Lake	D. W. Merrill,	2.00	....	10 ..
Chester,	Howland's	J. C. Howland,	2.00	A H	8 ..
Chittenango,	Dixon's	George Crandall,	1.75	A G	G ..
"	White Sulpur Spring,	Carsten W. Riecks,	4.00	....	.. ..
Cincinnatus,	Farmers	A. L. Smith,	1.00	A B	A ..
Clarksville,	Plank Road	Joseph Allen,	1.00	A B	A ..
Clay,	Clarendon,	W. Jerome Vreman	2.00	A J	I ..
Clayton,	**Hubbard's**	J. T. Hubbard,	2.50	....	.. ..
Clayville,	Murray	N. S. Hickox,	2.50	A I	7 ..
Cleveland,	Wilson's	A. M. Wilson,	....	....	.. ..
Clifton Park,	Rexford Flats	Hiram Parker,	1.50	A F	A ..
Clifton Sp.,	Clifton	Murray Caldwell,	2.00	A I	I ..
"	Sheldon	J. W. Sheldon,	1.50	A F	8 ..
Clyde,	Clyde	Cole & Brewster,	....	....	.. ..
"	Newman's	William Newman,	....	....	.. ..
Cobleskill,	Augustan	A. C. Smith,	....	....	.. ..
Cohoes,	City	J. Crocker,	....	....	.. ..
"	Miller	Frank Brown,	2.00	A I	I ..
Constantia,	Lake View	A. Cole & Sons,	1.50	A E	E 15
Cooperstown,	Carr's	L. A. Carr,	2.00	x	.. ..
"	Clinton,	Gordon Schermerhorn,	1.50	....	10 ..
"	Cooper S. R.	Coleman & Maxwell,	....	....	.. ..
"	Globe	S. M. Ballard,	2.00	x	.. ..
Corning,	American	Smith & Bacon,	1.50	A E	.. ..
"	Arcade	C. A. Terry,	2.00	....	6 ..
"	Minot	Fred'k Rothfuss,	....	....	.. ..
Cornwall,	Clark's S. R.	Josiah G. Clark,	....	....	.. ..
"	Roe's	James G. Roe,	....	....	.. ..
Cortland Village,	Dexter's	L. Dexter,	1.50	A E	.. ..
" "	**Messenger**	Wm. S. Copeland,	3.00	A I	J ..
Coxsackie,	Cummings'	Wm. W. Cummings,	....	....	.. ..
Crown Point,	Gunnison's	George Gunnison,	....	....	.. ..

NEW YORK.

TOWN.	HOTEL.	PROPRIETOR.			
Cuyler,	Cuyler	D. L. Pierce,	1.25	AE	C ..
Dansville,	Allen	George Swick,	2.00	AG	7 ..
"	American	Howe & Coon,			
Davenport,	American	E. C. Sheldon,	1.25	AD	C ..
Deerfield,	Smith's	Norman F. Smith,			
De Kalb,	Burnham's	John Burnham,			
Delhi,	American	R. D. W. Kiff,	2.00		
"	McDonald's	J. H. McDonald,			
Deposit,	Western	V. Huguiner,			
DeRuyter,	Taber's	Gilbert Taber,.			
Dobbs Ferry,	Archer Place	Stephen Archer,			
Dunkirk,	Avenue	C. Ward,	1.50	AB	A ..
"	Eastern	Walter Finkel,	2.00	....	10 ..
"	Erie	James Garraus,			
"	Farmers	T. M. Brick,	1.50	AD	D ..
"	Lake Shore	Robert Kenyon,	1.00	AA	A ..
Eagle Bridge,	Dalton	Daniel Randall,	2.00	AB	A ..
Earlville,	Jones'	Wm. H. Jones,			
East Chester,	Odell's	Stephen B. Odell,	2.50		
" Hampton,	Sea Spray	Wm. S. Gardiner,			
Eaton,	Burden's	Henry Burden,			
Edmeston,	Barton's	Samuel Barton,			
Elizabethtown,	American	Levi Ballard,	2.00	AH	E ..
Ellicottville,	Exchange	Frank Crawford,	2.00	AI	.. ..
Elmira.					
110 Lake St.,	Arbour	Haight, Jones & Co.	.00	E	.. ..
120 E. Water,	Bush's	W. Bush,			
408 E. Water	Continental	J. Bopp,			
523 R. R. Av.,	Delavan	R. Hunt,			
R. R. Av. & 3d	Fraziers	M, Bartholomew,	3.00	AM	.. ..
505 R. R. Av.,	Globe	G. A. Struppler,			
117 W. Water,	Pennsylvania	DeWitt Spence & Co.,	2.00	AI	I 18
....	Rathburns	E. R. Abbott,			
805 Canal,	Rolling Mill	H. Connelly,	1.00	....	7 ..
503 R. R. Av.,	Washington	G. Hummell,	2.00		
515 R. R. Av.,	Western	Jacob Schlosser	2.00	AC	C ..
113 W. Third,	Winslow's	J. T. Winslow,			
Esperance,	Union	D. L. Feathers,			
Evans Mills,	Burtis'	J. & S. Burtis,			
Fairport,	Fairport	Theron A. Holdridge			
Fayetteville.	McGuire's	Mrs. C. H. McGuire,			
Fire Island,	Surf S. R.	D. S. S. Sammis,			

NEW YORK.

TOWN.	HOTEL.	PROPRIETOR.			
Fishkill,	Kniffen's	John L. Kniffen,	2.00	A I	8 16
" Landing,	Fishkill	James Pettigrode,	1.50	A F F	..
" "	Rail Road	H. E. Travers,	....	....	..
Flatbush,	Nelson's	Benj. S. Nelson,	....	....	..
Flushing,	Flushing	E. B. Simmons,	....	....	..
"	Hennings'	Fred. Hennings,	....	....	..
"	Lowerre	Wm. Gale,	....	....	..
Fluvanna,	Sherwin	P. O. Sherman,	2.00	A I	I ..
Fonda,	European	T. Bush,	....	....	..
"	Johnson's	D. W. C. Johnson,	....	....	..
"	Union	Fisher Bros.,	....	....	..
Fort Edward,	Eldridge	W. H. Eldridge,	2.00	....	..
"	Millimans	H. C. Newton,	2.00	x	..
"	St. James	J. W. Moore,	2.00	A I	I ..
Fort Plain,	American	Josiah Zoller,	....	....	..
"	Montgomery Hall	Thomas Lumley,	2.00	A I	I ..
Fredonia,	Harrison	Joseph Brown,	2.00	A E E	..
"	Taylor's	Taylor Bros.,	....	....	..
Fulton,	Dexter	W. S. Cole,	1.00	A B A	..
"	Stevens'	D. W. Stevens,	....	....	..
Gallattinville,	Gallattinville	J. A. Spaulding,	1.50	....	5 ..
Gardiner,	Gardiner	John T. Upright & Son,	1.50	....	5 ..
Garrison's Landing,	Highland	G. F. & W. D. Garrison,	....	....	..
Geneseo,	American	Whittleton & Warren,	2.00	A H	.. ..
"	Globe	I. J. Stratton,	1.50	A E E	12
"	Robinson's	W. H. Robinson,	2.00	....	8 ..
Geneva,	American	P. Becker,	2.00	....	12 ..
"	Franklin	Sidney S. Mallory,	....	....	..
"	Geneva	Wm. Chipps,	1.50	A E D	..
Glens Falls,	American	George Pardoe,	2.00	x	..
"	New Hall	M. Bitely,	1.50	x	..
"	Rockwell's	Rockwell Bros.,	3.00	A L L	..
Gloversville,	Alvord's	C. G. Alvord,	2.00	....	10 ..
"	Mason	Wm. Howell & Son,	....	....	..
"	Palmer's	Robert Palmer,	1.00	....	6 ..
"	Scoville	J. W. Scoville,	1.50	A E E	..
Goshen,	Erie	James Thompson,	....	....	..
"	Occidental	J. E. Wickham,	....	....	..
Governeur,	Van Buren's	J. B. Van Buren,	....	....	..
Granville,	Central	L. B. Ranney,	2.00	....	8 ..
Great Valley,	Albright's	A. F. Albright & Co.	....	....	..

TOWN.	HOTEL.	PROPRIETOR.	
Greenbush,	Broadway	L. Slade,	....
Greene,	Chenango	F. E. Gillson,	2.00 .... 6 ..
Greenville,	Elliott's	Thomas Elliott,	....
Greenport,	Clark's	Mrs.MariaJ.Clark,	2.50 A 12 ..
"	Wyandank	Chas. C. Wright,	2,50 A x 12 ..
"	Wells'	J. Y. Wells,	....
Greenwich,	Greenwich	James Kennedy,	....
Guilderland,	Sloan's	Henry Sloan,	2.00 AG G ..
Guilford,	Guilford	John Bailey,	2.00 AF 6 ..
Hadley,	Kathan's	John A Kathan,	....
Hamburg,	Saunders'	Henry Saunders,	....
Hamilton,	Kelly's	John D. Kelly,	,.........
Hammond,	Taylor's	M. G. Taylor,	....
Hancock,	Hancock	C. B. Griffis,	2.00 .... 7 ..
Harford,	Shaver's	M. J. Shaver,	....
Hartwick,	Eldred's	R. & A.M.Eldred,	1.50 AE 6 ..
Havana,	Webster	M. J. Weaver,	2.00 AE E 15
Haverstraw,	National	Fred'k Bonnet,	2.00 AG G ..
Hempstead,	Hewlett's	Mrs.ElizaHewlett,	....
"	Pettit's	John B. Pettit,	,.........
"	Powell's	Chas. Powell,	1.50 AF 6 ..
Herkimer,	Allman's	T. Allman,	....
"	Mansion	F. Popper,	2.00 .... 10 ..
HighlandFalls,	Highland Falls S. R.,	George Stephens,	2.00 AI I ..
Hillsdale,	Hillsdale	Alex. Miller,	....
Holland,	**Holland**	W. S. Paul,	2.00 AI 5 ..
Homer,	Patten's	John Patten & Son,	....
Hoosick,	Phenix	Terry Wallace,	2.00 ....
Hornellsville,	Central	Andrew Edgett,	....
"	Nichol's	F. S. Nichols,	2.00 x ....
"	Osborn	W. Brainerd,	....
"	Simmons'	Wm. H. Simmons,	....
Howard,	Central	W. C. Bishop,	....
Hudson,	American	H. Thornton,	0.50 EC ....
"	Central	Henry S. Squires,	2.00 x ....
"	Farmers	E. Lasher,	1.00 AA A ..
"	Hudson	Walter Rogers,	2.00 x ....
"	Waldren's	Benj. H. Waldren,	2.00 AI H 16
"	Worth	Charles Miller,	3,00 x ....
Huntington,	Biggs'	George W. Biggs,	....
"	Suffolk	Samuel Hubbs,	....
Illion,	Osgood's	Philo Osgood,	2.00 AI ....
Islip,	Lake House	AmosR.Stellenwerf	3.00 A ....

NEW YORK. 45

TOWN.	HOTEL.	PROPRIETOR.			
Islip,	Somerset	George Westcott,	2.00	AI	I ..
Ithaca,	Clinton	S. D. Thompson,	....	....	.. ..
"	Freis	E. Ellis,	2.00	AG	7 ..
"	Ithaca	A. Sherman & Son,	3.00	....	.. ..
Jamestown,	American	J. B. Clark,	2.00	x	.. ..
"	Gifford	M. K. Hotchkiss,	2.50	x	.. ..
"	Jamestown	A. M. Shearman,	2.50	x	.. ..
"	Lake Shore	Frank L. Griffith,	2.50	....	12 ..
"	Sherwin	A. M. Sherman,	2.00	....	12 ..
"	Weeks'	Weeks Bros.	1.50	x	.. ..
Jamesville,	Cadogan	W. D. Clapp,	2.00	AF	7 ..
Jay,	National	L. W. Partridge,	1.50	AF	D 14
Jeffersonville,	Jeffersonville	Peter F. Bogert,	1.50	AE	E ..
Johnstown,	Rail Road	Gustin Laird,	2.00	x	.. ..
"	Sammonds'	M. E. Sammonds,	2.00	....	5 ..
"	Sir Wm. Johnsons	Waite & George,	2.00	x	.. ..
Jordan,	American	Cornell & Hovey,	2.00	AI	I ..
Keeseville,	Adirondac	L. F. Sprague,	....	....	.. ..
"	Ausable	M. J, Fields & Co.,	2.00	....	10 ..
Kinderhook,	Central	Griffin Mandeville,	2.00	AF	F ..
"	Kinderhook	Wm. Bradley,	2.00	....	7 ..
Kingston,	Eagle	H. W. Winnie,	....	....	.. ..
"	Humphey's	Horace Humphrey	2.00	....	9 ..
"	Merchants	I. Sailer,	....	....	.. ..
Knowersville,	Severson	J. Stafford,	....	....	.. ..
Lake Mahopac,	Gregory	L. H. Gregory,	....	....	.. ..
Lancaster,	American	John Raynor,	2.00	AI	7 ..
Lansingburg,	American	Alex. Smith, Jr.,	1.50	AE	E 14
"	Wilson's	Jesse P. Wilson,	....	....	.. ..
Le Roy,	Lampson	C, F. Gilson,	2.50	....	.. ..
Lewiston,	American	Hiram B. Cornell,	....	....	.. ..
Liberty,	Messiter's	Alfred Messiter,	....	....	.. ..
Little Falls,	Bradford's	N. A. Bradford,	2.00	x	.. ..
"	Girvan	John E. Allen,	2.00	x	.. ..
"	Hinchman	G, L. Bradley,	2.00	AI	I ..
Lockport,	American	W. Tenbrook & Son,	2.00	AI	I ..
"	Hovey	Jacob C. Hovey,	2.00	AI	I ..
"	Judson	R. W. Barr,	2.00	AI	I ..
Lowville,	Howell	S. B. Sahler,	2.00	AI	I ..
"	Kellogg's	K. C. Kellogg,	....	....	.. ..
Luzerne,	Rockwell's S.R.	G. T. Rockwell & Son,	2,00	AI	.. ..
Lyons,	Congress Hall	N. A. Langdon,	2.00	....	8 ..
"	National	L. Denchler,	1.50	AA	A ..

46 NEW YORK.

TOWN.	HOTEL.	PROPRIETOR.	
Madrid,	Smead's	D. D. Smead,	2.00 AI D ..
Malone,	Ferguson	A. R. Flanagan,	2.50 AK K ..
"	Hogle's	J. L. Hogle,	....
Malta,	Exchange	James V. Arnold,	....
Mamaroneck,	Sheldrake	W. H. Somers,	.... /. ..
Markhams Corners,	Metzger's	L. W. Metzger,	1.00 AD 6 ..
Margaretville,	Ackerley's	J. B. Ackerley,	2.00 AF F 16
Massena,	Bentley's	J. S. Bentley,	2.00 AE E ..
"	Hatfield's	Hatfield Bros.,	....
Mattituck,	Mattituck	B. F. Wells,	....
Mayville,	Mayville	J. R. Robertson,	2.00 AI 1 ..
"	Van Valkenburg	Mrs. H. Van Valkenberg,	1.50 AE D ..
Mechanicsville,	Saratoga	John G. Burnap,	2.00 AI .. ..
Medina,	Clark's	Aaron Clark, Jr.,	....
Mexico,	Hoyer's	L. H. Hoyer,	....
Middleburg,	Atchinson	E. D. Atchinson.	....
Middletown.	Exchange	W. L. McBride,	....
"	Grand Central	F. S. Betts,	2.00 AI I 18
"	Stage	Halsted Sweet,	....
"	Taylor	John Shearman,	....
"	Walkill	Robert Higham,	....
Millerton.	Clark's	N. G. Clark,	....
Moira,	Humphrey's	James Humphrey,	....
Monroe,	Monroe	Hollenbeck&Bush	....
Montgomery,	Empire	W. C. Lodge,	1.50 AE 6 ..
"	National	Hinkley Bros.,	2.50 AJ .. ..
"	Rail Road	James M. Marsh,	2.00 .... 8 ..
"	Wallkill	D. A. Shafer,	2.00 x .. ..
Monticello.	Mansion	Le Grand Morris	2.00 .... 10 ..
Mooers,	Junction	H. W. Lawrence,	....
Moravia,	Skinner's	C. A. & A. Skinner,	....
Moriches Centre.	Ketcham's	T. V. Ketcham,	2.00 AG G ..
" "	Long Island	Gilbert S. Terry,	2.00 AI H ..
Morris,	Louisville	W. H. Gardiner,	....
Morrisville,	Barker's	E. R. Barker,	2.00 .... 10 ..
Mt. Morris,	Wallace's	J. D. Wallace,	2.00 AG E ..
Mt. Vernon,	Mt. Vernon.	Theodore Gould,	2.00 .... 12 ..
Newark,	Hooper	T. S. Hooper,	2.00 AE 5 ..
" Valley,	Dimmick	Dimmick&Young,	2.00 AI 7 ..
NewBaltimore,	Rowe's	Mrs. Wm. H. Rowe,	....
New Brighton,	Pavillion S. R.	R. F. Cole,	....

NEW YORK. 47

TOWN.	HOTEL.	PROPRIETOR.		
Newburgh.				
17 Front St.,	Blizard	E. Schoonmaker,	1.00 x	.. ..
73 Front,	City	S. L. Gallinski,	2.00 x	.. ..
51 Front,	National	Wm.J.Hutchinson	0.50 E x	.. ..
....	Odell's	C. B. Odell,	'0.50 E x	.. ..
85 Vater,	Orange	J. E. Lasher,	3.00 A x	.. ..
Second cor. Front,	United States	Goodsell Bros.,	3.00	16 ..
Newcomb,	Mt. Pobley	C. S. Parker,	1.25 AF	D ..
NewHamburg	New Hamburg	MarvinVanAuden	2.00 AI	.. ..
New Paltz,	Saxton's	Abel Saxton,	2.00	.. ..
New Rochelle,	Huguenot	Robert S. Spurge,	3.00	.. ..
"	Neptune S.R.	S. C. Barr,	....	.. ..
New Suffolk,	New Suffolk	Wm. McNish,	1.50 AF	E ..
New York City.				
Fifth Av. cor. 24th St.	Albemarle	T. & I. Hagaman,	2.00 E	.. ..
834 Broadway,	Anthony	Charles A.Merritt,	1.00 E	5 ..
4thAv.cor.24th,	Ashland	H. H. Brockway,	3.00 AN	N ..
" "	"	"	1.00 EF	.. ..
221 Broadway,	Astor	Allen & Dam,	1.00 E	.. ..
137 Fulton,	**Belmont**	J. H. Clay,	0.50 EC	.. ..
395 Bowery,	Bowery	Lawrence R. Kerr	....	.. ..
Madison Av. cor. 58th,	Branting	....	3.50 A	25 ..
Broadway cor. Canal,	Brandreth	Kerr & Slader,	1.00 E	.. ..
225 Fifth Av.	Brunswick	Mitchell,King&Co.	3.00 E	.. ..
5thAv.cor.50th,	Buckingham	Gale, Fuller & Co.,	1.50 E	.. ..
272 West,	Central	Waterman&Brown	0.50 EC	.. ..
Broadway & 8th,	City	M. E. Dwinelle,	2.00 A	12 ..
"	"	"	1.00 EF	.. ..
64 Union Sq.,	Clarendon	Charles H.Kerner,	5.00 A	.. ..
Canal&Centre,	Earle's	Earle Bros.,	3.00 AM	.. ..
64 Whitehall,	Eastern	James C. Betts,	1.00 E	.. ..
3d Av. & 24th,	Elliott	Richard Dyer,	2.00 AI	14 21
1 Chatham,	French's	T. French & Bro.,	....	.. ..
48NewB'wery,	Grant	L. Barlow,	50 E	3 ..
671 Broadway,	Grand Central	H. L. Powers,	3.00 A	.. ..
4th Av. & 41st	" Union	G. F. & W. D. Garrison,	1.00 E	.. ..
Madison Sq.	Hoffman	C. H. Read,	....	.. ..
17 Park Row,	International	J. Van Brimmer,	1.00 E x	.. ..

NEW YORK.

New York City.	HOTEL.	PROPRIETOR.			
46 Chatham,	Leggett's	Leggett & Storms,	75 E x		
E. Broadway & Catharine,	Marion	D. W. Halman,	50 E	3	
39 Courtland,	Merchants	Wm. G. Schenck,			
586 Broadway,	Metropolitan	Breslin, Purcell & Co.,			
5 Courtland,	National	A. J. Halliday,	1.00 E		
Bowery & Broome,	Occidental	J. F. Darrow,	0.75 E		
606 Broadway,	Revere	T. J. Coe & Son,	1.00 E x		
B'way & 42d,	Rossmore	Charles E. Leland,	4.00 A		
"	St. Cloud	Rand Bros.,	1.50 EK		
B'way & 11th	St. Denis	Wm. Taylor,			
515 Broadway,	St. Nicholas	Samuel Hawks & Co.,			
754 Broadway	Sinclair	A. L. Ashman,	1.00 E		
58 Chatham,	Smith's	Samuel Smith,	75 EC		
197 Wash'gt'n,	Smith & McNells'	Smith & McNell,	75 E		
679 Broadway,	Southern	H. E. Billings,	2.00 A	12	
5 Union Sq.,	Spingler	T. J. Coe,	3.00 A	18	
760 Broadway,	Stacy	Stacy & Nelson,	1.00 E	5	
1186 "	Sturdevant	Louis & Geo. S. Leland,	4.00 A	28	
65 Bowery,	Summit	George Ruckert,	0.50 E	3	
665 Broadway,	Tremont	Caddagan & Hasbrouck,	1.00 EF		
16 Union Sq.,	Union Square	A. J. Dam & Son,	1.50 E		
Fulton&Water,	United States	Truman&Peabody,	1.00 E x		
246 8th Av.,	West Side	Edward A. Roher,	75 EC	6	
IrvingPl.&16th	Westminster	Chas. B. Ferrin,	1.50 E		
Niagara Falls,	Cataract S. R.	Whitney Jerauld & Co.,	4.50 x		
"	Exchange	Francis McNulty,	2.00 x		
"	Falls S. R.	James A. Young,	2.50 x		
"	International S. R.	Jas. T. Fulton, Jr.,	4.50 x		
"	Niagara,	Lewis & Davie,	2.50 AI	14	
"	Spencer	A, Cluck,	3.50 AO	O	
"	Union	Edward Lane,	2.00 x		
Northport,	Northport	Selah Smith,	2.00 A x		
Northville,	National	Ash & Conkling,			
Norwich,	American	Beebe & Medbury,			
"	Spaulding's	Ira Spaulding,			
Nunda,	Eagle	Christian Smith	2.00	14	

NEW YORK. 49

TOWN.	HOTEL.	PROPRIETOR.			
Nunda,	Livingston	W. Wood,	1.50	AF	F ..
Nyack,	Palmer's	Rebecca Palmer,	2.50	x	.. ..
"	Pavillion	A. P. Smith,	....	....	.. ..
"	Rockland Co.	Wm. Wessels,	2.00	x	.. ..
"	Smithsonian	J. Lyon,	....	....	.. ..
Ogdensburg,	Baldwins	Levi Stevens,	2.00	x	.. ..
"	Commercial	J. S. Steel,	2.00	x	.. ..
"	Johnson	H. I. Goodno,	2.00	....	7 ..
"	National	William Owen,	1.50	AH	E ..
Olean,	American	J. Good,	1.00	x	.. ..
"	Moore's	M. V. Moore,	2.00	x	.. ..
"	Olean	Geo. Van Campon,	2.00	x	.. ..
Oneida,	Allen's	Frederick Allen,	2.00	....	12 ..
"	Eagle	Frank Foote,	2.00	x	.. ..
"	German	J. Hople,	1.50	x	.. ..
"	Madison	R. M. Northrup,	2.00	x	.. ..
Oneonta,	Hathaway's	Leonard Hathaway	....	....	.. ..
Orient,	Orient Pt. S. R.	M.B.Parsons&Co.	....	....	.. ..
Oriskany Falls,	Sargent's	A. Sargent,	1.50	AF	.. ..
Oswego.					
23 W. Seneca St.	American	Samuel W. McCay,	1.00	....	5 ..
125 E. First,	Cleveland	Charles E. Betts,	1.00	AAA	..
... W. First,	Doolittle	J. G. Bement,	3.00	x	.. ..
82 E. First,	Empire	Turner & Foyette,	1.00	AD	5 ..
....	Fitzhugh	Samuel Coy,	2.00	x	.. ..
Bridge&W.8th,	Gotie	Michael Keeler,	1.00	....	6 ..
67 E. First,	Hamilton	S. H. Stacy,	2.00	x	.. ..
... E. Bridge,	Johnson	R. W. Johnson,	1.50	AF	C ..
196 E. 10th,	Mansion	Geo. Rozell,	2.00	AH	G ..
... W. Bridge,	Merchants	C. H. Philipps,	1.00	....	5 ..
... Water,	Ontario	Charles W. Ott,	2.00	x	.. ..
59 E. First,	Rail Road	Mrs.E.A.Murdick,	1.00	....	5 ..
... E. First,	Reciprocity	James Otis,	1.00	....	4 ..
... W. First,	St. Nicholas	C. J. Robinson,	1.50	AF	E 12
Otego,	Marsh's	Henry Marsh,	....	....	.. ..
Otisville,	Green's	O. B. Green,	....	....	.. ..
Ovid,	Park	Daniel Clough,	....	....	.. ..
Owego,	Ah-wa-ga	Raymond & Son,	2.50	x	.. ..
"	Central	B. J. Davis,	2.00	x	.. ..
"	Owego	Patrick Hickey,	1.50	x	.. ..
Oxford,	St. James	Daniels & Van Wagenen,	2.00	AI	I ..
Palmyra,	Eagle	Wm. H. Throop,	2.00	x	.. ..
"	Palmyra	C. B. Stewart,	2.00	x	.. ..
"	Rail Road	Thomas L. Quaife,	2.00	x	.. ..

NEW YORK.

TOWN.	HOTEL.	PROPRIETOR.			
Parish,	Carley	W. H. Marsh,	2.00	AH	G ..
Patchogue,	**Roe's**	Anstin Roe,	2.50	AI	I ..
"	West End	H. J. Bishop,	2.00	AG	H ..
Pawling,	Pawling	Arnold & Ross,	2.00	AI	7 ..
Peekskill,	Continental	Geo. H. Sutton,	2.00	x	.. ..
Penn Yan,	Central	Charles Kelly,	2.00	AH	H ..
"	Farmers	A. D. Farr,	1.00	....	4 ..
"	Mansion	Oliver C. Knapp,	2.00	....	5 ..
Perrysburg,	Campbell	C. Campbell,			
Petersburg,	Moses'	Chas. J. Moses,			
Philadelphia,	Eagle	Jas. H. Washburn			
Phelps,	Globe	Geo. W. Decker,	1.50	AF	E 10
"	Ticknor's	J. H. Ticknor,	,		
Piermont,	Ackerman's	Thos. J. Ackerman			
Pine Lake,	Canada Lake	Joseph Sherman,	2.00	AI	I 18
Pine Plains,	Myers	W. S. Dibble,	2.00	AF	E ..
Pittsford,	Phenix	Mrs. Wm. Hicks,			
Plattsburg,	Cumberland	E. Averill,	2.00	....	11 ..
"	Fouquets	A. A. Smith,	3.00	x	.. ..
"	Witherills	D. McBride,	2.50	x	.. ..
Poestenkill	Poestenkill	J. P. Southard,	1.50	AC	5 ..
Port Byron,	National	William Gallt,	2.00	....	10 ..
Port Chester,	Putnam	James Shea,	1.50	....	7 ..
Port Henry,	Pease's	Chrrles B. Pease,			
Port Jefferson,	Port Jefferson	Holmes W. Swezey	2.00	x	.. ..
"	Smith's	Thomas Smith,	2.00	....	11 ..
"	**Townsend**	C. H. Davis,	2.00	AI	G ..
Port Jervis,	American	I. M. Reeves,	1.50	x	.. ..
"	Delaware	G. S. Reddington,	2.00	x	.. ..
"	Fowler	W. J. Scott,	2.50	AJ	10 ..
"	Globe	Wm. Dargin,	1.25	AB	B ..
"	Minnesink	Alex. Gordon,	1.50	x	.. ..
"	National	Samuel J. Wood & Son,	2.00	AH	H ..
Port Leyden,	Desbrough's	Desbrough & Co.,			
Potsdam,	American	S. D. Bridge,	2.00	x	.. ..
"	Elm St.	A. J. Holmes,	2.00	E	x .. ..
"	Matteson	Matteson & Riper,	2.00	x	.. ..
PotsdamJunc.	American	Amos Bicknell,	2.00	x	.. ..
"	Ives	Adam Holmes,	2.00	......	.. ..
"	Whitney	S. B. Phelps,	2.00	AI	11 ..
Poughkeepsie.					
275 Main St.,	Anson's	R. Anson,			
Main St. Ldg.,	Exchange	V. Hoffman,	2.00	....	10 ..

NEW YORK 51

	HOTEL.	PROPRIETOR.			
Poughkeepsie					
... Mill,	Northern	L. L. Hutchins,	2.00	 10	..
Market & Cannon,	Park	Hinkley & Co.,	3.00 AJ	J	..
163 Main,	Stanwix Hall	McGau&McCaffrey	....	....	..
Prattsville,	Elm Cottage	C. E. Richtmeyer,	3.00	 10	..
Prospect,	Union	Wm. P. Dodge,	2.00 AE	E	..
Pulaski,	Gray's	William H. Gray,	....	....	..
Randolph,	Helmes'	Byron Helmes,	....	....	..
Redwood,	Copley's	William Copley,	....	....	..
Remsen,	Dawson's	Geo. W. Dawson,	....	....	..
Rhinebeck,	Tremper's	Tremper Bros.	....	....	..
Richfield Sp.,	American	Wm. P. Johnson,	2.00	 12	..
"	International	W. L. Darrow,	2.00	 12	..
"	Spring	T. R. Proctor,	4.00	....	..
Riverhead,	Long Island	John P. Terry & Son,	2.00 A1	I 15	
"	Suffolk	John Corwin,	2.00 A	....	..
"	United States	Louisa Court,	1.75 AG	9	..
Rochester.					
... Mill St.,	Brackett	Samuel M. Hildreth & Co.,	3.00 AM	....	
12 N. Water,	British American	Harry Mairch,	1.25 AH	7	..
Court&St.Paul	City	E. Bouton,	....	....	..
28 Exchange,	Clinton	I. Ashley & Co.,	2.00	 12	..
R. R. Ave. & Mill,	Congress Hall	James Terry,	3.00	....	
Main & Elm,	Farmers	N. P. Wilbur,	1.50	 8	..
280 N. St. Paul,	Genesee Av.,	John C. Moore,	1.50 AC	B	..
Lower Falls,	Glen	S. Bennett & Son,	....	....	..
10 Platt,	Mechanics	Michael Cummins,	1.00	 5	..
State cor. Brown,	NorthAmerican	Patrick Burns,	1.50 AE	E	..
Mill & Centre,	Toronto	Daniel Desmond,	1.00 AB	A	..
R, R. Ave. & State,	Waverly,	Walbridge & Maxwell,	2.00	....	
Rome,	Commercial	Hiram Nellis,	2.00 x	....	
"	Mohawk	T. C. Wilds,	....	....	
"	Northern	Wm. Beck,	1.50 AE	D	..
"	Seymour	Harvey Edmonds,	....	....	
"	Stanwix Hall	A. J. Sink,	2.00	 11	..
"	Willett	Ira L. Reed,	2.00 x	....	
Rosendale,	DuBois'	James J. DuBois,	....	....	
Roslyn,	Givens'	Jacob Givens,	....	....	

NEW YORK.

TOWN.	HOTEL.	PROPRIETOR.			
Ronses Point,	Clinton	James Pearson,	2.00	AI	8 ..
"	Massachusetts	James Shaw,	2.00	....	14 ..
"	Thompson's	Mrs. Mary Thompson,	....	....	.. ..
Rye,	Central	W. D. Beck,	2.00	AI	I ..
"	Irving	C. Winkenbach,	2.50	x	....
"	Rye	James Morrison,	2.00	x	....
"	Rye Beach	J. Robinson & Co.,	3.50	x	....
Sag Harbor,	Nassau	Mrs. Alfred Oakley	2.00	x	....
Salamanca,	Krieger's	A. H. Krieger,	....	....	..
Salem,	Potter's	Horace Potter,	....	....	..
Sandy Creek,	Salisbury's	B. F. Salisburg,	2.00	AI	G ..
Sand Bank,	Albion	Isaac N. Gurley,	1.00	AB	....
Sandy Hill,	Coffee	N. W. Clark,	2.00	AI	I ..
"	Rexford	Homer Rexford,	1.50	AF	E ..
Sand Lake,	Crooked Lake	James M. Mosher,	2.00	AF	E 15
Saratoga Sp.	Albion	W. T. Gibson,	1.50	AF	F 16
"	American	Wm. Bennett,	....	....	..
"	Arlington	Marvin Snyder & Bros.	....	....	..
"	Clarendon	Chas. E. Leland,	....	....	..
"	Commercial	J. T. Bryant,	2.00	AI	....
"	Congress Hall	Cook & Hathorn,	....	....	..
"	Elmwood Hall	Wm. H. Lewis,	2.00	AJ	J 20
"	Empire	L. Parris,	....	....	..
Saugerties,	Central	Mrs. M. Clark,	....	....	..
"	Conger's	Jacob L. Conger,	....	....	..
Savannah,	Savannah	John A. Fowler,	....	....	..
Sayville,	Bedell's	Isaac Bedell, M.	3.00	AI	I ..
"	Foster's	A. D. Foster,	1.50	AE	E ..
Schenectady,	American	N. Timeson,	1.50	AE	6 10
"	Freeman	George Brown,	....	....	..
"	Germania	C. Wiencke,	....	....	..
"	Merchants	L. Sickler,	2.00	AF	F 16
"	Myers	G. Luckhurst,	1.50	AE	A ..
Schenevous,	Schenevous	Dewitt Chamberlain,	2.00	AI	....
Schodack,	Masonic Hall	Lewis & Westfall,	1.00	....	7 ..
Schoharie,	Parrott's	Sidney & Parrott,	....	....	..
Schroon Lake Village,	Ondawa	John D. Burwell,	2.50	AJ	K ..
"	Leland's	Wm. G. Leland,	....	....	..
Schuylerville,	Schuylerville,	Gannon Bros.,	....	....	..
Scottsville,	Scottsville	C. H. Barrett,	1.50	....	5 ..

NEW YORK. 53

TOWN.	HOTEL.	PROPRIETOR.		
Searsville,	City	A. R. Vanderlyne,	1.00	5 :
Seneca Falls,	Franklin	Otis L. Fisher,	1.50	7 ..
"	Globe	John Woodmansee	2.00 x	...
"	Hoag	Geo. Hayt & Son,	2.00 x	...
SharonSprings,	Eldridge's	Eldridge & Son,	....	....
"	Fether's S. R.	C. B. Fethers,	2.00 AI	I ..
"	Pavillion	J.H.Gardner & Son	....	....
"	United States	J. J. Anthony,	....	....
Sheldon,	Glasser's	Frank Glasser,	....	....
Sherburne,	Medbery's	George Medberry,	....	....
Sherman,	Sherman	Stanley & Son,	1.00 AH	5 ..
Sidney Plains,	Delaware	Mrs. E. C. Curtis,	1.75 AH	G ..
Sinclairville,	Sylvester	Henry Sylvester,	....	....
Sing Sing,	American	E. H. Disbrow,	2.50 x	...
"	Phenix	C. Dailey, Jr.,	2.00 x	...
"	St. Cloud	J. H. Steneck,	2.00 x	...
Skaneatles,	Packwood	F. A. & E. A. Andrews,	....	....
Smithboro,	Armstrong's	Jas. R.Armstrong,	....	....
Smyrna,	Messenger's	M. K. Messenger,	....	....
Sodus,	Sodus	L. Whitney,	....	....
S.Oyster Bay,	Kilian's	George Kilian,	2.00 AI J	20
"	S. Oyster Bay	R. D. Macomber,	2.50 AN	14 ..
Spring Valley,	Spring Valley	John L.Haring,	2.25 AJ	10 ..
Springville,	Oyer's	Andrew Oyer,	....	....
Spring Water,	Alger's	D. P. Alger,	2.00 AG	G ..
Staatsburg,	Valley	Charles F. Martin,	1.75 AH	H ..
Stillwater,	Fowler's	Wm. N. Fowler,	....	....
Stony Brook,	Smith's	Mrs. Jane Smith,	2.00 AH	7 ..
Strykersville,	Merchants & Farmers	Frank Glaser,	1.00 A	4 ..
Stuyvesant,	Stuyvesant	W. H. Clapp,	2.00....	10 ..
"	" Falls	W. C. Smith,	2.00 AI	.. ..
Suffern,	Gallaway's	R. F. Gallaway,	....	....
Suspension Bridge,	Atwoods Western	George E. Brock,	2.50 AI	.. ..
" "	Monteagle	Wm. P. Monroe,	....	....
" "	N. Y. Central	Felix Massoiy,	2.00 AI	14 ..
Syracuse.				
4 Everson Block,	Central	J. C. Snow,	2.00 AI	I ..
85 E.SenecaSt.	Cheesebrough's	Silas J. Cheesebrough,	1.00 AB	.. ..
68 Franklin,	Emmett	A. McGurk,	1.50	8 ..
Salina & Genesee,	Empire	Rockwell & Carpenter,	3.00 AL	....

NEW YORK.

Syracuse.	HOTEL.	PROPRIETOR.			
11 Franklin,	Everson	Hasbrouck & Myers,	2.00	x	....
Washington & S. Salina,	Globe	Dickerson&Austin	3.00	x	....
36 N. Salina,	Onondaga	E. T. Talbot,	1.00	AA	....
35 W. Fayette,	Oswego	Nathan Sayles,	1.00	AA	....
E. Washington,	Remington	Dickinson & Austin,	3.00	x	....
S. Salina,	Syracuse	Wm. C. Gage & Co.	2.50	x	....
24 W. Fayette,	**Temperance**	E. T. Talbot,	2.00	AI	....
E. Washington & Warren,	Vanderbilt	John L. Cook & Sons,	3.00	AM N	..
47 S. West,	Westervelt	John D. Ryan,	1.50	AE 5	..
Taberg,	Central	Patrick Kelley,	1.00	 5	..
Tarrytown,	Revere	Wm. Perry,			
Taughannock Falls,	Taughannock	P. H. Thompson,	2.00	AI I	..
Thurmans	Thurmans	John Loveland,	2.00	AF E	..
Ticonderoga,	Fleming's	Wm. S. Fleming,			
Tonawanda,	Excelsior,	W. W. Yager,	2.00	 8	..
Trenton Falls,	Trenton Falls	M. Moore,	4.00	 21	..
Troy.					
130 Congress,	Eagle	John S. Eldred,			
426 River,	Frommann's	Herman A. Frommann,			
River cor. Ferry,	International	Marston & Abey,	2.00	AG G	17
Broadway,	Nelson	H. K. Bush,	2.00	AI J	..
"	"	"	0.75	ED	....
456 River,	Northern	G. P. Cozzens,	2.00	AI 7	..
River & First,	Troy	J. W. Stearns,	3.00		
19 Sixth,	Waverly	S. V. R. Young,	2.00	AH 7	..
Trumansburg,	Phenix	A. P. Sears,	2.00	AI J	..
"	Trembley	Leroy Trembley,	2.00	AI 12	20
Unadilla,	Brick	Charles Bishop,			
Union,	Major	N. D. Hoag,	2.00	 10	..
Utica.					
Genesee St.	American	Browell & Towne,			
17 Whitesboro,	Dudley	Chas. H. Stevens,	2.00	 14	..
18 Whitesboro,	Globe	O. F. Hulse & Bro.	2.00	AI I	..
Fay & Columbia,	Midland	A. M. Geer,	2.00	 8	..
31 Oneida,	Morning Walk	Wm. E. Jones,	1.00	AB B	..
Valley Falls,	Valley Falls	Robert Wood,			:
Victor,	Victor	Geo. W. Peer,	2.00	AH F	..
Waddington,	Clark's	Wm. Clark,	1.25	AC A	..
"	Union	Mrs. W. Oliver.			

NEW YORK.

TOWN.	HOTEL.	PROPRIETOR.			
Warwick,	National	T. H. Demerest,	2.00	....	10 ..
"	**Wawayanda**	Thos. J. Randall,	2.00	....	7 ..
Warsaw,	Hatch	E. W. Cook,	2.00	AG	G ..
Waterford,	Fox's	Wm. H. Fox,	2.00	....	7 ..
"	Morgan	Thos. Van Derkar,	2.00	....	7 ..
Waterloo,	Franklin	A. S. Holenback,	1.00	AC	A 10
"	Grove	Jacob Smith,		....	.. ..
"	Towsley	L. Goodman,		....	.. ..
Watertown,	American	A.M.Harris & Son,	....	....	.. ..
"	Crowner	Wilder Bros.		....	.. ..
"	Hanchett	Mrs.W.C.Hanchett	....	....	..
"	Harris	Helmer & Parrish,	1.50	AE	7 ..
"	Woodruff	Buck & Sanger,	3.00	AL	14 ..
Waterville,	American	Andrew Young,		....	.. ..
Watkins	Fall Brook	A. M. Baker&Son,	2.00	AI	I ..
"	Glen Park,	E. C. Frost,	3.00	AJ	J ..
"	Jefferson	Blaisdell & Hill,		....	.. ..
Watson,	Fenton's	C. Fenton,	2.00	AI	J 21
Waverly,	Waverly	Walbridge & Maxwell,	2.50	AI	.. ..
Wayland,	Pfaff's	Adam Pfaff,		....	.. ..
Weedsport,	Ketcham's	J. W. Ketcham,	1.50	AE	E 15
"	Mansion	Henry Stickle,	2.00	AG	D 12
Wellsville,	American	J. B. Stannard,	1.50	....	5 ..
"	Fassett's	I. W. Fassett,	2.00	AI	7 ..
"	Onondaga	H. W. Dowdney,	1.50	....	7 ..
Westfield,	Minton	J. H. Minton,	1.75	AF	F ..
West Lebanon,	Dunham	B. P. Dunham,	1.25	AB	B ..
" Sand Lake,	Seymour	Sam'l D. Seymour,	1.25	AD	D ..
West Troy,	Patten's	Patten & White,		....	.. ..
Whallonsburg,	Davis'	.... Davis,	1.50	AE	7 ..
Whitehall,	Allen's	Mrs.MaryA.Allen,	....	....	.. ..
White Lake,	Mansion	D. B. Kinne,	2.00	....	10 ..
White Plains,	**Roe's**	Josiah Roe,	2.50	AJ	I ..
Williamstown,	Curtis'	D. J. Curtis,		....	.. ..
Williamsville,	Eagle	D. Sawtell,	1.00	....	5 ..
"	Mansion	Joseph Seitz, Jr.,	1.00	AA	A ..
Wolcott,	Whiting's	Julius Whiting,		....	.. ..
Woodsburg,	Pavillion	N. Weed,		....	.. ..
"	Neptune	Martin Wood,	2.00	....	10 ..
Yonkers,	Getty	Wm. H. Doty,	3.00	AM	M ..
Youngstown,	Barton	Alex. Barton,		....	.. ..
Youngsville,	Dutcher's	Thomas Dutcher,		....	.. ..

NEW JERSEY.

TOWN.	HOTEL.	PROPRIETOR.				
Absecom,	Murphy's	Elmer Murphy,				
Allentown	Bird's	N. W. Bird,				
Atlantic City	Alhambra	Robert B. Leeds,				
"	American	L. Kinley,				
"	Congress Hall	G. W. Hinkle,				
"	Sea Side	Evans & Haynes,				
"	St. Charles	J. Wooton,				
"	Kuehnle's	Louis Kuehnle,	2.50	A K	L	..
"	United States	Brown & Woelpler,				
Barnegat,	Clarence	Chas. Roeder,	2.00	A I	I	20
Basking Ridge,	Washington	Charles A. Moore,	2.00	A H	G	16
Belvidere,	American	A. Lanback,	2.00	....	10	..
"	Belvidere	H. H. Fisher,	2.00	A H	H	18
Bergen Point,	La Tourette S. R.	J. Bowman,				
Bernardsville,	Travellers Home	Jas. P. Baird,	1.50	A	9	..
Boonton,	Park	Alfred A. Snyder,	2.00	A G	G	..
"	United States	P. H. Brown,	2.00	A I	J	..
Bordentown,	Bordentown	Levi Davis,	2.00	....	11	..
"	City	H. H. Trout,	1.75	....	9	..
Bound Brook,	Meehan's	John Meehan,				
Branchville,	American	Geo. J. Bowman,	2.00	A I	7	14
Bricksburg,	Talmago	Walter Beancy,	2.00	A H	H	18
Bridgeton,	City	Samuel Peacock,	2.00	....	8	..
Budds Lake,	Forest S. R.	A. Brownson,				
Burlington,	Haynes'	Mrs. John B. Haynes,				
Camden,	Archer's	Samuel Archer,				
"	Parson's	S. Parsons,				
"	W. Jersey	Campbell & Bro.				
Cape May S. R.,	Atlantic	John McMakin,	2.50	A J	J	..
"	Congress Hall	Jacob F. Cake,				
"	Delaware	James Mecreay,				
"	Merchants	William Mason,	3.00	A N	N	..
"	National Hall	Aaron Garretson & Son,				
Columbus,	Atkinson's	E. Atkinson,				
Cranberry,	American	Mrs. M. J. Bowne,				
Dover,	Mansion	J. B. Jolley,	2.50	x		...
Egg Harbor,	New York	Louis Knehnle,	1.50	A F	F	..
Elizabeth,	Schwartz'	Louis Schwartz,	1.00	E x		....
"	Sheridan	George Miller,	3.00	A K	K	20
Englewood,	Ackerman's	John Ackerman,				
"	Palisade M't'n S. R.	D. S. Hammond,				
Englishtown,	Union	James Smock,	1.50	A I	5	..

TOWN.	HOTEL.	PROPRIETOR.		
Fairview,	Kelly's	Daniel Kelly,		
Farmingdale,	Hyer's	T. Hyers,		
Flemington,	Crater's	George F. Crater,		
Franklin Furnace,	Franklin	Geo. W. Rhodes,	1.50	5
Freehold,	Davis'	William Davis,		
"	Union	E. C. Richardson,	2.00	9
Gloucester,	Gloucester	H. Mullen,	1.50 AE	E
"	Mansion	P. J. Gilligan,	3.00 AN	15
Hackensack,	McCracken's	Wm. McCracken,		
Hackettstown,	Trimmer's	David M. Trimmer		
Hoboken,	Park	F. Bruckbauer & Co.		
"	Sinclair	George Taddiken,	0.50 EC	
Hope,	American	H. W. Rundell,		
Jersey City,	Taylor's	Lyman Fisk,	1.00 EG	
Keyport,	Poole's	William J. Poole,		
Lambertville,	Corson's	John Corson,		
Long Branch	Mansion	Wm. L. McIntyre,	4.00 AR	R
"	West End	Presbury & Hildreth,		
Metuchin,	Raritan	John Smith,	1.00 AB	7
"	Van Sickles	A. Dunn,		
Millburn,	Smith's	C. H. Smith,		
Millstone,	Hancock's	Geo. Hancock,		
Millville,	Millville	Geo. P. Doughty,	2.00 AJ	I
Montclair,	Rossiter's	Thos. Rossiter,		
Montville,	Montville	Wm. Ranouse,	2.00	12
Morristown,	Farmers	George Hedden,	1.50	8
"	Mansion	B. C. Guerin,	2.00 AH	I
"	United States	B. F. Sherwood,	2.00	
Newark,	Commercial	John McConel,	1.00	6
"	Continental	C. W. Carpenter,		
"	Newark	J. H. Hare,	1.00 EG	
New Brunswick,	City	Silas Hall,		
"	Moores	Moore & Dunn,		
"	Parks'	F. H. Parks,	2.50 AF	F
Newton,	Howell's	S. Howell,		
Norwood,	Norwood S. R.	J. Bowman,		
Orange,	Hall's	Thomas Hall,		
"	Central	J. W. McChesney,		
Passaic,	Eutaw	Alfred Speer,	1.50 AD	D
Patterson,	Boonton Branch	Francis Blair,	1.50	10
"	Exchange	J. W. Baughman,	1.50 AE	8

NEW JERSEY.

TOWN.	HOTEL.	PROPRIETOR.		
Patterson,	Passaic	John P. Zeluff,	2.00 AJ	....
"	United States	J. Bunn,		
Pemberton,	Reeve's	Joseph J. Reeves,		
Perth Amboy,	Moore's	Moore & Sutphin,		
Philippsburg,	Apgar's	George L. Apgar,		
Plainfield,	City	Chris. Van Arsdale	2.50 AL	L ..
"	Laing's	John W. Laing,		
"	Park,	M. B. Curtis,	3.00 x	....
Princeton,	Nassau	E. E. Rittenhouse,		
Rahway,	Chamberlain's	Wm. S. Chamberlain,		
"	Melick	James T. Melick,	2.00 AG	G ..
Raritan,	Raritan	Peter S. Petty,	2.00 AI	G ..
Red Bank,	Atkins'	James M. Atkins,		
Salem,	French's	Samuel French,		
Sharpstown,	Farmers & Drovers	Jacob Beck,	2.00 AI	I ..
Somerville,	City	C. Van Arsdale,		
South Amboy,	Rail Road	Nelson W. Taft,	1.00	6 ..
South River,	Walker's	Benj. B. Walker,		
Spottswood,	Snowhill's	Lydia A. Snowhill		
Tenafly,	Truman's	J. L. Truman,		
Toms River,	Chadwick's	William Chadwick,		
Trenton,	National	Early & Mount,	2.50 AJ	I ..
"	Trenton	P. Katzenbach,	4.00	
Tuckahoe,	Star	Thomas Buzby,	1.50 AH	7 ..
Tuckerton,	Carlton	G. H. Vannote,	2.00 AI	I ..
Vineland,	**Vineland**	H. L. Manning,	2.00 AJ	D ..
Vincentown,	Atkinson's	Benj. Atkinson,		
Washington,	Hoagland's	U.V.C. Hoaghland		
Woodbridge,	De Graw's	William De Graw,		
Woodbury,	Paul's	Joseph Paul,		
Woodstown,	Ford's	Charles C. Ford,		

TOWN.	HOTEL.	PROPRIETOR.		
Alleghany,	Central	W. H. Howard,	2.00	12
"	Harlan's	David Harlan,		
"	Hoffman's	Wm. Hoffman,		
"	Morgan	John Grant,	2.00	7
Allentown,	American	J, F, Newhard,	2,50 AL	L
"	Eagle	Levi Hottenstein,		
Altoona,	Brant	Mme. C. Shahik,		
"	Fountain Inn	A. Franklin Mower		
"	Mountain City,	Philip Faddle		
"	St. Charles	J. Fitzharris,		
"	Wm. Tell	John O'Neil,		
Apollo,	American,	Mrs. Jane Smith,		
Archibald,	Union	Christian Linde,		
Ashland,	Mansion	E. Bensinger,	1.50 AH	6
"	Repplier,	C. S. King,		
"	Union	Charles Culp,	2.50 AI	8 16
Ashley,	Ashley,	Philip McKearman,		
Athens,	Jordan's	George Jordan,		
Auburn,	Moyer's	Joseph K. Moyer,		
Beaver,	Clark's	John B. Clark,		
Beaver Falls,	Brackens	T. H. Bracken,		
Bedford,	Purcell's	J. M. Purcell,		
"	Steckman's	Valentine Steckman,		
Bellefonte,	Bush's S. R.	W. H. Wilkinson & Co.,	3.00 AK	
"	Garman's	Daniel Garman,		
Bethlehem,	Eagle	George Hoppes,	3.00 AN	L
"	Old Moravian Sun	C. T. Smith,	2.50 AL	
Blairsville,	Union	George Wilkinson	1.25 AH	5
Bloomsburg,	Koon's	W. B. Koon,		
Brady's Bend,	Mitchell's	Thomas Mitchell,		
Bristol,	Clossom's	J. W. Clossom,		
Brockwayville,	Rail Road	B. Frank Townley,	1.50	7
Brookville,	Clements	A. S. Scribner,	2.00	7
Brownsville,	Krepps'	John B. Krepps,		
Butler,	Jack's	Benjamin Jack,		
Carbondale,	Elm Tree	Solomon Arnold,		
"	Flynn's	Michael Flynn,		
"	Keystone	Jas, C. Morrison,		
Carlisle,	American	John J. Ringwalt,		
"	Bentz	George Bentz,	1.00 A x	
"	Exchange	Francis Leron,		
"	Franklin	John Keep,		

PENNSYLVANIA.

TOWN.	HOTEL.	PROPRIETOR.		
Carlisle,	Letort	Thos. Lindsay,		
"	Mansion	Barney Riley,		
Catasaqua,	Harte's	H. S. Harte,		
Centralia,	Peiffer's	Wm. Peiffer,		
Chambersburg,	Indian Queen	John Fisher,	1.50 A H	7 ..
"	Miller's	John Miller,		
"	Washington	E. S. Shank,	2.00	.... 10 ..
Chester,	American	Jas. Harvay,		
"	City	Paul Klotz,	2.00 A F	F 16
"	Delaware	D. Brown,		
"	Morris'	Benj. Morris,		
"	Steamboat	John Goff,	1.50 A F	7 ..
"	Washington	H. Abbott, Jr.,		
Clearfield,	Shaws	N. R. Shaw,		
Coatesville,	Stevenson	Vandever&Phipps	2.00	.... 11 ..
Columbia,	**Black's**	Joseph H. Black,	2.00 A I	I ..
"	Farmers	John Hinkle,		
"	Riverside	S. H. Lockard,		
Connellsville,	Smith's	Mrs. B. R. Smith,		
Conshocton,	O'Brien	Michael O'Brien,		
Coplay,	Biege's	Jackson Biege,	1.50 A H	F ..
Corry,	Central	O. McNally,	1.50 A E	6 ..
"	Downer	Wm. H. Shaw,	3.00 A L	....
Danville,	City	Adam Geringer,	2.00 x	....
"	Montour	James L. Riehl,	3.00 x	....
"	Union	JosephM.Geringer		
Dauphin,	Gayman's	Jacob Gayman,		
Delaware Water Gap,	Delaware W. G.	L. W. Brodhead,	4.00	.... 21 ..
Downington,	Rail Road	M. McFadden,		
Doylestown,	Miller's	Thomas P. Miller,		
Duncannon,	Washington	Wm. Scheibley,	2.00 A H	D ..
Easton,	United States,	Samuel Hayden,	3.00 A M	N ..
Ebensburg,	Blair's	John A. Blair,		
Emporium	Sweazey's	C. Sweazey,		
Emlenton,	Moran	T. A. Moran,		
Erie.				
State & North Park St.,	Ellsworth	S. M. Ellsworth,		
18th & Peach,	Erie City	O. R. Clarke,		
5th & French,	Farmers	John Boyle,	1.50	.... 6 ..
1300 Peach,	Morton	Kelly & Edwards,		
....	Park Place	Davis & Bone,		
....	Reid	S. V. Harris,	.	

PENNSYLVANIA.

	HOTEL.	PROPRIETOR.		
Erie.				
State near 11th,	United States	Wm. Kahoe,		
Everitt,	United States	F. Snyder,	1.25 AC	C ..
Franklin,	Exchange	Cornelius Tyson,	2.00 x	....
"	Grant	H. B. Kentner,	1.50 x	....
"	National	J. H. Whann,	1.50 AF	D ..
"	United States	H. T. Willoughby,	2.00 x	....
Freeport,	Mitchell's	John Mitchell, Jr.,		
Gettysburg,	Eagle	George Hoppes,	2.00 AJ	J ..
Girard,	Evan's	Joshua Evans,		
Great Bend,	Kilron's	Michael Kilron		
Greensburg,	Laird	James Borlin,	2.00	7 ..
Greenville,	Huber's	Adam Huber & Son,		
Hanover,	Smith's	Ambrose Smith,		
Harrisburg.				
....	Bolton's	G. I. Bolton,	3.00	
....	Bulls Head	J. Shaffner,	1.50	6 ..
....	Bomgardner	M. Shelley,		
....	Franklin	Frank Dietrich,	1.50 AF	D ..
....	Kirkwood	Kirkwood & Bro.,	3.00 x	....
....	Lochiel	Geo. W. Hunter,	3.00	
....	State Capitol	Wm. Thompson,		
....	United States	W. H. Eminger & Co.,		
Hawley,	Seidler's	Frederick Seidler,		
Hazleton,	Central	James Fitzpatrick,	2.50 AK	K ..
"	Hazleton	Conrad Seiple,	2.50 x	....
"	Mansion	E. C. Vincent,	2.00 x	....
Hollidaysburg,	American	Daniel K. Reamey,	2.00 AI	I ..
Honesdale,	Allen's	M.B.&W.R.Allen,	2.00 x	....
"	Ball's	Henry Ball,	2.00 x	....
"	Coyne's	M. Coyne,		
"	Kiple's	R. W. Kiple,	2.00 x	....
Hughesville,	Baker's	David Baker,		
Huntington,	Boyer's	J. G. Boyer,		
"	Miller's	John S. Miller,		
Indiana,	Sweeney's	M. Sweeney,		
Jamestown,	Cornwell	C. S. Hamilton,	2.00 AI	I 16
Jersey Shore,	Jersey Shore	J. H. Callahan,	2.00 AG	G 17
Johnstown,	Merchants	Luther Martin,	2.00 AH	7 ..
"	O'Connell's	P. O'Connell,		
Kingston,	McPike's	P. McPike,		
Kitanning,	Dougan's	A. Dougan		
"	Walker	James B. Walker,	2.00 AF	F ..

TOWN.	HOTEL.	PROPRIETOR.	
Lancaster.			
N. Queen St.,	Cadwell	H. L. Barnet,	....
35 W. King,	Cooper's	W. J. Cooper,	2.50 A L 14 ..
....	City	Sidis & Jeffrey,	....
12 W. King,	Cross Keys	M. Kreider,	....
122 N. Queen,	Franklin	Geo. Schlott,	....
....	Franke's	H. Franke,	....
242 N. Queen,	Keystone	Ream & Groff,	1.25 A E D ..
....	Stevens	Wilson & Son,	....
Lebanon,	Eagle	A. F. Seigrist,	2.00 AI I 19
"	Lebanon Valley	E. M. Boltz,	2.00 AF F 12
Lewisburg,	Cameron	Geo. S. Burr,	2.00 AI J ..
Lock Haven,	Fallon	J. Schuyler, Jr.,	2.00 ....
"	Montour	Houseal & Krom,	2.00 AI I 18
Marietta,	Florey's	Mrs. Sarah Flory,	....
Mahanoy City	Mansion	W. F. Smith,	2.50 x ....
MauchChunck,	American	H. J. Woodring,	3.00 AL ....
Meadville,	Scowden's	Joseph Scowden,	....
Media,	Charter	A. Watrous,	2.25 AH H 18
Middletown,	Dolson's	Valentine Dolson,	....
Mifflintown,	Wills'	Jacob Wills,	....
Millersburg,	Washington	Henry Heikel,	1.50 .... 6 ..
Milton,	Huff's	Mrs. J. M. Huff,	....
Minersville,	Exchange	John Mock,	2.00 AI 7 ..
Monongahela,	Sheplar's	James P. Sheplar,	....
Montrose,	Harrington	M. J. Harrington,	....
Morrisville,	Carlisle's	John Carlisle,	....
Moscow,	Dixon's	Lyman Dixon,	....
Mount Joy,	Weaver's	Lewis Weaver,	....
Muncy,	United States	M. Welliver,	....
New Castle,	Cochran	Ed. H. Long,	1.75 AH H ..
"	Leslie	Stoughton&Duffy,	2.00 ....
Newport,	Miller's	B. F. Miller,	....
Newtown,	Temperance	S. R. Willard,	....
Norristown,	Farmers & Mechanics	Francis Kile,	....
"	Montgomery	Mrs. M. L. Carter,	2.00 AJ ....
"	Penn Farmer	D. Hartranft,	....
North East,	Dawson's	George W. Dawson,	....
Northumberland,	Johnson's	Mrs. Julia Johnson,	....
Oil City,	Duncan	Washington Alden	2.00 AI I ..
Oxford,	Oxford	J. Menough,	....

PENNSYLVANIA.

TOWN.	HOTEL.	PROPRIETOR.		
Parker,	Frisbee's	F. H. Frisbee,	3.00	
Petroleum Centre,	Central	L. Davis,		
Phenixville,	Phenix	James Keeler,		
Philadelphia.				
812 Market St.,	Alleghany	A. Beck,	2.00 A J	.. ..
1220 "	Allen	Robert Wallis,	2.00 A	11 ..
Chestnut above 5th,	American	S. M. Henlings,	3.00 A x	.. ..
Elm Av. & 52d,	Atlas	John Crump,	1.00 E	.. ..
4 Chelton Av.,	Avenue House	John Haywood,	1.00 E	5 ..
41st & Oregon,	Belmont	R. W. Clements,	1.50 E x	.. ..
Market & 11th,	Bingham	Curlis Davis,	3.00 A x	.. ..
Broad near Mt. Vernon,	Broad St.	B. F. Grubb,	1.00 E	.. ..
926 N. Front,	Bulls Head	Chas. J. Vowinkle	2.00 A	10 ..
Chestnut & 15th,	Colonade	J. Crump,	3.50 A x	.. ..
111 N. Broad,	Columbia	Lewis H. Worman	2.50 A J	.. ..
826 Market,	Commercial	Henry Schlichter,	2.00 A J	J ..
Chestnut&9th	Continental	J.E.Kingsley&Co.	4.50 A x	.. ..
610 Annapolis,	Farmers	Samuel Beckett,	1.75 A	9 ..
S.W. cor.Vine & Franklin,	**Franklin Sq.**	R. S. Bailey & Son	3.00 A J J	22
Chestnut & 9th,	Girard	McKibbin, Vosburg & Co.,	3.50 A x	.. ..
Girard & LancasterAv.	GrandExposition	M. Riley, M.	2.00 E	.. ..
Seventh & Chestnut,	Guys	F. A. Miller,	1.50 E x	.. ..
Walnut cor. 33d	Hotel Aubrey	Jas. T. Stover, M.	2.00 E x	.. ..
Walnut above 9th,	Irving	R. Stokes' Sons,	3.00 A N	21 ..
Broadway near Chestnut,	La Pierre	J. B. Butterworth,	3.00 A x	.. ..
1619 Market,	Market	Daniel B. Butler,	2.00 A I	J ..
919 Chestnut,	Markoe	H. M. Beidler,	3.00 A x	.. ..
Fourth near Market,	Merchants	Cummings, Case & Co.,	3.00 A x	.. ..
413 N. Sixth,	Montgomery,	Geo. W. Jackson,	2.00 A J	12 ..
Delaware Av. & Market,	Ridgeway	J. B. Butterworth,	.. ..	.. ..
709 Arch,	St. Cloud	Geo. W. Mullin,	3.50 A x	.. ..
Chestnut&10th,	St. Stephens	Thomas Ashton,	3.50 A x	.. ..
....	Tacony Resort	Chas. J. Vowinkle,	3.00	15 ..

64 PENNSYLVANIA.

Philadelphia.	HOTEL.	PROPRIETOR.		
327 Vine,	Tiger	Samuel Grubb & Son,	2.00 A	....
Chestnut near 7th,	Washington	Geo. J. Bolton,	3.00 A x	....
Philippsburg,	Roberts	Mrs. A. Howarth,	....	.. ..
Pittsburg.				
139 Water St.,	Baldwin	P. F. Drhew,	2.00	7 ..
419 Liberty,	Bavarian	Lang & Schmidt,	....	.. ..
Third Ave. & Smithfield.	Central	J. G. Barr & Sons,	3.00 x	....
401 Liberty,	Lundy's	John Lundy,	....	.. ..
First Ave. & Smithfield,	Monongahela	J. McDonald Crossan,	4.00 x	....
Duquesne & Seventh,	Robinson	R. E. Robinson,	2.50 AJ	14 ..
Liberty & 11th,	Rush	M. Rush,	2.50 AJ	I ..
"	"	"	0.75 EE	.. ..
Wood & 3d Av.,	St. Charles	Chalfont & Newkirk,	2.50 x	....
PennAv.&6th	St. Clair	C. P. Bailey,	2.50 AK	L ..
Grant&4thAv.,	St. Nicholas	Miller & Co.,	2.50 x	.. ..
Irwin Ave.,	Union Depot	Elias J. Unger,	3.50 AO	O ..
Pittston,	Eagle	Joseph Godfrey,	2.00 AI	....
Pottstown,	Madison	E. R. Plankinton,	....	.. ..
"	River	C. Missimer,	....	.. ..
Pottsville,	Lion	A. Reinhart,	2.00 x	....
"	Middle Ward	L. Ditmer,	....	.. ..
"	Penn Hall	W. W. Reed,	2.50	.. ..
"	Rail Road	W. Burke,	....	.. ..
Reading.				
Fourth & Penn St.,	American	Behm & Weaver,	....	.. ..
1637 Centre Av.	Centre Avenue	Geo. D. Davis,	2.00 AI	I ..
Cherry & 6th	City	J. W. Adam,	....	.. ..
751 Chestnut,	Girard	Andrew Henke,	1.00	5 ..
Penn & N. 6th,	Keystone	Eli S. Fox,	2.00 AI	....
Penn & S. 3d,	Merchants	L. M. Gerhart,	....	.. ..
427 Penn,	United States	Levan W. Krick,	1.50	8 ..
Scranton,	Coyne	P. H. Coyne,	1.50 AH	7 ..
"	Lackawanna	A. S. Patter,	2.50 A x	....
"	Wyoming	Gardner & Koon,	2.50 A x	....
"	Forest	U.G.Schoonmaker	2.00 AH	H ..
Scrubgrass,	Gregory	Wm. H. Buckley,	2.00 AE	E 15
Shamokin,	United States	Wm. F. Kitchen,	....	.. ..
Shickskinny,	Yaple's	Henry J. Yaple,	2.00 AI	I ..

TOWN.	HOTEL.	PROPRIETOR.	
Shippensburg,	Shermans	Isaac A. Quigley,	
Somerset,	Somerset	E. A. Flick,	2.00 AH G 1
Stroudsburg,	American	D. L. Pisle	
"	Burnett S. R.	James C. Griggs,	
Sunbury,	City	E. T. Drumheller,	2.00 AI I ..
"	Clement	P. S. Burrell,	2.00 AI 8 14
Susquehanna,	Benson	Abmrose Benson,	
Tamaqua,	United States	Wm. H. Kintzle,	2.00 AI I ..
Tarentown,	Marvin	George Truby,	1.50 AC D ..
Titusville,	Bateman's	Bateman & Bros.,	
"	Weil's	Weil Bros.,	
Towanda,	Means	Thos. R. Jordan,	
Troy,	Troy	V. M. Long,	2.00 AI 11 ..
Tyrone,	Ward's	P. F. McIntyre & Co.,	2.00 AI G ..
Washington,	Fulton	Little, Melvin&Co.	
Watsontown,	Cooner's	J. R. Cooner,	2.00 .... 5 ..
"	Mansion	John B. Gilbert,	2.00 AI 7 ..
Waverly,	Bradford	R. H. Fish,	1.50 AE B ..
West Chester,	Mansion	N. T. Hayes,	2.50 AL K ..
White Haven,	Lehigh	M. B. Posten,	2.00 AI J ..
"	White Haven	T. Smith,	2.00 AI J ..
Wilkesbarre,	Bristol	Laycock Bros.	2.50 x .. ..
"	Exchange	E. C. Wasser,	
"	Luzerne	S. Bristol,	
"	White Horse	Mrs. Perrin,	2.00 x .. ..
"	WyomingValley	J. B. Stark,	3.00 x .. ..
Williamsport,	American	Lewis Martin,	2.00 x .. ..
"	Central	Miller & Co.,	2.00 x .. ..
"	City	Sloanaker&Gains,	2.50 x .. ..
"	Crawford's	Wm. Crawford,	2.50 AK K ..
"	Hepburn	Wm. Dennison,	2.50 x .. ..
"	Henry's	Henry Bower,	2.00 x .. ..
"	Herdick	P. Herdick,	3.00 x .. ..
"	United States	Harman & Miller,	
York,	Kindig	Elisha Brown,	1.25 AD 7 ..
"	Motter	I. F. Gross,	
"	National	H. H. Elliott,	2.50 .... 15 ..
"	Pennsylvania	John Lenheart,	1.50 ....
"	St. Charles	J. Leidy,	
"	Washington	Elias Eyster,	

DELAWARE.

TOWN.	HOTEL.	PROPRIETOR.		
Dover,	Capitol	Wm. C. Fountain	2.50 AN 12	..
"	Schaick's	Geo. C. Schaick,	....	.... ..
Georgetown	Eagle	James H. Wood,	2.00 AI G	..
Lewes,	United States	Mrs. S. C. Wells,	2.50 x	....
Milford,	Cole's	Amos Cole,	2.00 AE E	15
"	Milford	Justus Lowery,	2.00	9 ..
Newark,	Lewis'	John E. Lewis,	2.00 x	....
New Castle,	Delaware	George S. Beckett,	2.00 AH	7 ..
"	Gilpin	George Whitfield	....	.... ..
Odessa,	Lippincott's	B. F. Lippincott,	1.50 x	....
Seaford.	Patterson's	S. G. Patterson,	1.50 x	....
Smyrna,	Millington's	G. A. Millington,	2.00 x	....
Wilmington.				
....	City,	Jacob B. Hyatt,	....	.... ..
....	Clayton,	H. W. Sawyer,	....	.... ..
....	Logan,	Fred. Schmidt,	....	.... ..
Front St.,	Pennsylvania	Wm. L. Gilbert,	....	.... ..
205 Market,	Washington,	Hugh Horner,	2.00 AI	I 14
Tatnall & Second St.,	White House	Caleb Miller,	....	.... ..

MARYLAND.

TOWN.	HOTEL.	PROPRIETOR.		
Annapolis	City	J. R. Walton,	....	.... ..
"	Maryland	W.H.Gorman&Co.	....	.... ..
Baltimore.				
Calvert & Franklin St.,	American	Mrs. R. Fairchild, & Son,	1.50 AF F	16
Calvert & Fayette,	Barnum's	Barnum & Co.,	....	.... ..
Baltimore near Laight,	Carrollton	R. B. Coleman,	....	.... ..
Eutaw & Baltimore,	Eutaw	Wm. W. Leland,	4.00 AR	R 42
Calvert & Fayette,	GuysMonument	S. C. Little,	....	.... ..
5th near Howard,	Howard	Judd & Allen,	2.50	.... ..
180 Pratt	Maltby	C. R. Hogan,	2.50 AM L	..
"	"	"	1.00 EG	....
Fayette & St. Paul,	Mansion	L. Albertson,	1.50	.... ..
158 Franklin,	Pennsylvania	Wm. Delphey,	1.50 AG F	..

Baltimore.	HOTEL.	PROPRIETOR.	
45 w. Fayette,	Rennert's	R. Rennert,	... ...
24 N. Gay,	Rose	Patrick McGuire,	... ...
Monument Sq.,	**St. Clair**	W. H. Clabaugh	3.00 A P 18 ..
Cambridge,	Cambridge	Thomas & Cook,	1.50 A H G ..
"	Central	T. James Frazier,	1.50 A H G ..
Chestertown,	Hall's	John Hall,	1.50 A I 7 ..
"	Voshell	S. V. Farson,	2.00 A H H 18
Cumberland,	City	Mrs. Julia Adams,	... ...
"	Queen City	E. Mareau,	... ...
"	St. Nicholas	J. Newcomer,	... ...
Easton,	Paragon	Mrs. Julia A. Hall,	... ...
Elkton,	Falls'	William Falls,	... ...
Ellicott City,	**Howard**	Josiah Graves,	2.25 A J I ..
Frederick,	Dill	H. H. Power,	... ...
Frostburg,	Lynch's	Cornelius Lynch,	... ...
Hagarstown,	Antietam	H. H. Fowler,	1.75 A G 6 ..
"	Franklin,	G. G. Middlekauff,	2.00 A I I ..
Hancock,	Gillese's	Thomas Gillese,	... ...
Havre DeGrace,	United States	John P. Adams,	1.50 A H 7 ..
Port Deposit,	Hill's	William A. Hill,	... ...
Princess Anne,	Washington,	Wm. P. Rider,	2.00 .... 9 ..
Ridgeley,	Mancha's	H. S. Mancha,	1.25 A B A ..
Rising Sun,	Maryland	William Grason,	1.50 A H 7 ..
Snow Hill,	Washington	John B. Nock,	1.50 A H E ..
Salisbury,	Peninsula	John Tracy,	1.50 A H .. ..
Westminster,	City	F. I. Wheeler,	2.50 A I I 16
Williamsport,	Taylor's	Wm. E. Taylor,	2.00 A H 7 ..

WASHINGTON D. C.

TOWN.	HOTEL.	PROPRIETOR.	
7th & Penn Av.,	American	John B. Scott,	2.00 A I I 18
Vermont Ave.,	Arlington	T. Roessle & Son,	... ...
Penn Ave.,	Continental	F. J. Mesick,	2.50 A I I ..
14th & F,	Ebbitt	C. C. Willard,	... ...
15th & I,	Gray's	J. A. Gray,	... ...
13th & E,	Greason	Wm. Greason & Son	1.50 E ... ..
Penn Ave.	Metropolitan	J. A. Jordan & Co.,	... ...
1413 Penn,	Owen	Jordan & Gordon,	1.00 E ... ..
Penn & 3d,	Parkinson	A. Parkinson,	2.00 .... 10 ..
13th & D,	Snow	Samuel Hunt,	3.00 .... 18 ..
Penn & 6th,	St. James	Woodbury & Duren	.... E ... ..
Indiana & 2d,	Tremont	F. P. Hill,	2.50 A L L ..
Penn & 14th,	Willards	John F. Cake,	... ...

VIRGINIA.

TOWN.	HOTEL.	PROPRIETOR.	
Afton,	Afton	S. H. Goodloe & Co.	2.00 A H H
Alexandria,	City	Wm. H. Chapman & Bro.,	2.00 A H H ..
"	Mansion	James Green,	3.00 A L L ..
"	Tontine	Cooney & Bro.,	....
Amherst, C. H.	Central	M. H. Miller,	1.50 .... 5 ..
Appomattox,	Hix	E. G. Hix,	1.50 A F F ..
Bristol,	Virginia,	Nickels & Wood,	2.00 A L 10 ..
Buford,	Harris'	J. O. Harris,	2.00 A H H 16
Burkesville,	South Side	Wm. T. Flippin	2.50 A K K ..
Charlottesville,	Farrish	John M. Page & Co.	2.50 A J J 20
Christianburg,	Noell's	R. J. Noell,	....
Covington,	McCurdy's	McCurdy Sisters,	2.00 A F E ..
Danville,	Exchange	Julius Saunders,	2.00 A G G ..
"	Paxton	N. L. Wade,	2.00 A I 10 ..
Dublin,	Painter's	Painter & Caddall,	....
Edenburgh,	Murray's	Mrs. M. A. Murray	....
Fairfax C. H.,	Chapman's	W. R. Chapman,	1.50 A F F ..
"	Tyler's	H. B. Tyler,	....
Farmville,	Randolph	Charles Briggs,	2.50 A K .. ..
Fincastle,	Luster's	John Luster,	....
Fredericsburg,	Exchange,	John M. Reamer,	2.50 .... 12 ..
Front Royal,	Waverly,	Forsyth & Bro.,	2.00 A F F 17
Gordonsville,	Jennings'	John R. Jennings & Bro.,	....
"	St. John's	Snowden Yates,	2.00 .... 9 ..
Halifax C. H.,	Butt's	Thomas B. Butt,	2.00 A I I ..
Hillsville,	Elliott's	C. G. Elliott,	1.00 A A 5 ..
Hampton,	Barnes'	J. J. Barnes,	2.50 A J J ..
Holston,	Warley's	John W. Warley,	1.00 A A .. ..
Leesburg,	Reamer's	James Reamer,	2.00 .... 10 ..
Lexington,	National	A. A. Pitman,	2.50 A K I ..
Liberty,	Liberty	W. R. Terry,	....
Louisa C. H.,	Louisa	Benj. F. Trice,	....
Lynchburg,	Norvell	Holt & Terry,	....
"	Piedmont	Woolling Bros.,	....
"	Tyree,	J. A. Campbell,	....
"	Warwick	W. H. Rose,	1.50 A E E ..
"	**Washington**	George A. Myers,	2.25 A I J 20
Manchester,	Beattie's	Robert Beattie,	....
Mannington,	United States	Richard Parish,	2.00 A I I ..
Matthews,	Sliets'	Geo. E. Sliet & Bro.	....
Meherrin Sta.,	Davis'	Davis & Co.,	....
Newbern,	Bixbie's	M. E. Bixbie,	2.00 A H H ..

VIRGINIA. 69

TOWN.	HOTEL.	PROPRIETOR.	
Norfolk,	Atlantic	R. S. Dodson,	3.00 ....
"	Goode,	A. J. Manning,	1.50 x ....
"	Greene	B. Peddle,	1.50 x ....
"	Mansion	R. F. James,	1.50 x ....
"	Morrisett's	T. Morrisett,	00 E x ....
Nottoway C. H.	Blendon	James S. Gillian,	2.00 AI I 16
Old Pt.Comfort,	Hygia	H. Phoebus,	....
Petersburg,	**Bollingbrook**	Brown & Pettit,	2.50 AK K ..
"	City	S. A. Plummer,	3.00 AL L ..
"	Virginia	Mrs.S.V.Kennedy,	1.50 AH E ..
Princess Anne,	Rock Hall	J. H. Coffee,	2.00 AJ I ..
Portsmouth,	**American**	Mrs. C. Y. Diggs & Son,	2.00 .... 12 ..
"	Peabody's	James Little,	....
Richmond.			
Main & 12th St.,	American	J. N. Ballard,	2.00 AF F 17
Franklin & 14th,	Exchange	J. L. Carrington,	....
1320 East Main,	Merchants	V. I. Mountcastle,	2.00 .... 10 ..
912 Main,	Park	J. S. Dodson,	2.50 .... 12 ..
12th near Main,	St. James	T.W.Hoenniger,	3.00 AM .. ...
Rocky Mount,	Early's	G. W. B. Hall,	2.00 AH G ..
Rural Retreat,	Boyer's	Dr. H.Q.A. Boyer,	2.00 AH G 15
Salem,	Duval	Messrs Williamson & Co.,	2.50 AK 12 ..
"	Barnett's	Barnett & Lear,	2.00 AI ....
Staunton,	Miller's	Mrs. M. A. Miller,	....
Suffolk,	Swett's	Chas. L. Swett,	....
Timberville,	Timberville	M. M. Helbert,	2.00 AJ 8 ..
Warrenton,	Warrenton	James H. Maddox,	....
West Point,	News	W. D. Pollard,	2.00 AH 7 ..
Williamsburg,	City	I. Lamb,	2.50 AK K ..
Winchester,	Grim's	L. T. F. Grim,	....
"	Taylor	N. M. Cartmell,	2.50 AL L ..
Woodstock,	Welsh's	Charles Welsh,	....
Wytheville,	Crockett's	S. S. Crockett,	2.00 AJ I 16
"	Hancock's	L. D. Hancock,	2.00 AG G 15
Yellow Sulphur Spring,	Y. S. Spring	J. J. & J. Wade,	....

WEST VIRGINIA.

TOWN.	HOTEL.	PROPRIETOR.			
Berkeley Sp.,	Florence,	Charles Green,	2.50	AI	9..
Bridgeport,	West Virginia	W. C, Fitzhugh,			
Charlestown,	Owings'	Dr. C. H. Owings,	2.00	AG	G 18
Clarksburg,	Walker's	Samuel Walker,	2.00	AI	J..*
Fairmount,	Coombs'	H. S. Coombs,			
Grafton,	National	G. W. Ward,			
Harpers Ferry,	Mountain View	Geo. W. Green,	2.00	AJ	I..
Lewisburg,	Moore's	W. W. Moore,			
Martinsburg,	Berkeley	A. P. Shutt & Son,			
"	Everitt	Wm. Rutledge,			
"	Stewart	J. Johnson,	2.00	AI	I..
"	Shenandoah	John Teller,			
Morgantown,	Wallace's	James C. Wallace,			
Parkersburg,	Concordia	Andrew Als,			
"	National	John Kelly,	1.50	AE	5..
"	United States	Mrs. F. Brunswig,			
Piedmont,	Simms	J. P. A. Entler,	2.00	....	10..
West Union,	Davis'	Louis T. Davis,			
Wheeling.					
Main & 10th St.,	Grant,	Lewis&Woodmans	2.50	AL	M..
....	Lingaman's	L. Lingaman,			
....	Neuhart's	Henry Neuhart,			
1300 Water,	Stamm	Henry Stamm,	2.00	....	10..
White Sulphur Springs,	W. S. Springs	Geo.L.Peyton&Co.			

NORTH CAROLINA.

TOWN.	HOTEL.	PROPRIETOR.			
Ashville,	Eagle,	E. T. Clemmens,	2.00	....	10..
Beaufort,	Front Street,	W. Street,			
"	Atlantic,	G. W. Charlotte,			
Charlotte,	Charlotte,	J. Hollis & Son,	2.00	AI	I..
"	Mansion,	H. C. Eccles,			
Clinton,	Clinton,	Everitt Peterson,	2.00	AI	G..
Concord,	American,	N. Slough,			
"	Reed's,	Reed & Morris,			
Durham,	Watson's,	J. W. Watson,			
Edenton,	Bond's,	Sam'l T. Bond,	2.00	....	10..
"	Woodard's,	Richard Woodard,			
Enfield.	Enfield,	Peter Forbes,			

NORTH CAROLINA.

TOWN.	HOTEL.	PROPRIETOR.			
Fayetteville,	Fayetteville,	A. Overbaugh,			
"	Exchange,	W. Draughon,			
Flemington,	Brothers',	Mrs.M.E.Brothers,			
Goldsboro,	Goldsboro,	W. R. Barringer,			
"	Humphrey,	Silas P. Wright,			
Greensboro,	Benbow's,	D. W. Benbow,	2.50	A L	L ..
"	Planter's,	Mrs. L. A. Rees,	1.50	A H	G ..
"	Rees',	J. T. Rees,			
"	Yarboroughs',	E. A. Yarboroughs,	2.00	A H	F 17
High Point,	Jarrill's,	M. Jarrill,			
Hillsboro,	Orange,	L. L. Hassall,			
Kinston,	Bagby,	W. R. Becton,	2.50	A K	I ..
"	St. Charles,	W. L. Oast,			
Kittrels,	Davis',	Mrs. W. F. Davis,			
Lexington,	Perry's,	Eli Perry,	2.00	A I	G ..
"	Lexington	John S. Sowers,	2.00	....	10 ..
Lincolnton,	Johnson's,	B. S. Johnson,	2.00	A I	10 ..
Marion,	Chapman's,	George Chapman,	1.50	A H	E 12
"	Fleming,	M. B. Teague,	2.00	A H	G 12
Morgantown,	**Mountain,**	J. M. HAPPOLDT,	2.00	....	11 ..
"	Walton,	John C. Mallard,	2.00	A I	I ..
Newberne,	Merch'ntsClub,	W. L. Palmer,	2.00	A J	.. ..
Raleigh,	Central,	Charles H. Thomas,	2.00	....	.. ..
"	Exchange,	Mrs. Rosa Rowe,	2.00	A I	9 ..
"	National,	C. S. Brown,			
"	Yarbrough,	G. W. Blacknell,	3.00	A N	N 32
Reidsville,	**Labarbe's,**	A. P. LABARBE,	2.00	A I	10 ..
Salisbury,	Boyden,	Mrs. Dr. Reeves,	2.50	A I	H ..
Statesville,	Jackson's,	N. A. Jackson,	2.00	A I	D ..
Tarboro,	Adams',	O. F. Adams,	2.50	A I	H ..
Warrenton,	Norwood,	W.J.Norwood&Co.,	2.50	A K	K ..
Washington,	Raynor's,	W. Raynor,			
Weldon,	Emry's,	Southall & Style,			
Wilmington,	Manning's,	E. W. Manning,	2.50	A K	L ..
"	Purcell,	J. R. Davis,			
Winston,	Wilson,	P. A. Wilson,			

SOUTH CAROLINA.

TOWN.	HOTEL.	PROPRIETOR.		
Abbeville,	Abbeville,	Jacob Miller,	2.00	.... 7 12
Bamberg,	Cedar Springs,	J. J. Getsinger,	2.00 AG	....
Charleston.				
Meeting-st., n'r Hayne,	Charleston,	E. P. Jackson&Co.,	4.00 AS	....
190 King,	Forrest,	L. G. Pratt,	2.00 AJ	I ..
284 King,	Hilbers,	Mrs. Hilbers,	....	..
69 Broad,	Mansion,	Mrs. R. C. Finney,	2.00 AI	I ..
Queen&M'eting Mills',		Mrs. Kinloch,	....	..
353 King,	National,	Mrs. H. M. Baker,	1.50 AH	F ..
Me'tin nr Hazel,	Pavillion,	Geo. T. Alford&Co.,	3.00 AP	....
252 King,	Waverly,	Kennedy & Ruff,	2.50 AN	15 ..
Cheraw,	Cheraw,	D. J. Gasherie,	2.50	.... 10 ..
Chester,	Nicholson's,	Mrs.W.M.Nichols'n	....	..
Columbia,	Central,	....	2.00 AHH	..
"	Columbia,	William Gorman,	3.00	....
"	National,	Robert Joiner,	....	..
"	Rose's,	W. E. Rose,	2.50 AI	I ..
"	Washington,	Mrs. S. E. Stratton,	....	..
Darlington,	Floyd's,	John Floyd,	....	..
Georgetown,	Dorrill's,	Mrs. A. D. Dorrill,	2.00 AI	J 20
Greenville,	Mansion,	Calnan & Roath,	3.00 AN	N ..
Pendleton,	Pendleton,	....	2.00 AI	9 ..
Sumter,	Davis',	Chas. W. Davis,	3.00 AN	N ..
Spartanburg,	Palmetto,	A. Tolleson,	....	..
Walhalla,	Walhalla,	D. Bieman,	....	..
Winnsboro,	Winnsboro,	A. A. Morris,	2.50 AI	I 18

GEORGIA.

TOWN.	HOTEL.	PROPRIETOR.		
Acworth,	Litchfield's,	E. S. Litchfield,	2.00AI	I ..
Adairsville,	Central,	John C. Martin,	2.00	.... 10 ..
Albany,	Bennett's,	W. G. Bennet,	4.00	.... 20 ..
Americus,	Barlow,	Wiley Jones,	2.50	.... 13 ..
Athens,	**Newton**	A. D. Clinard,	2.00 A	....
Atlanta,	Air Line,	J. L. Keith,	2.00 AF	F 15
"	American,	....	1.50 AF	F 17
"	Cannon's,	Mrs. M. E. Cannon,	2.00	.... 10 ..
"	Kimble,	G. McGinley,	....	..
"	Markham	James E. Owens,	....	..
Augusta,	Augusta,	Fred Mosher,	3.00 A	15 ..
"	Central,	Mrs.W.M.Thomas,	3.00 AMM	..
"	Globe,	Patrick May,	....	..
"	Planters',	B. P. Chatfield,	....	..

GEORGIA.

TOWN.	HOTEL.	PROPRIETOR.	
Brunswick,	Blain's,	W. S. Blain,	....
"	City,	Dart & Fahm,	2.50 A ....
"	Globe,	T. MAHONEY,	2.00 .... 10 ..
Bainbridge,	Shawn's,	John Shawn,	2.00 .... 10 ..
Cartersville,	Tennessee,	Mrs. T. Sumner,	2.00 AHII ..
Columbus,	Rankins,	Mrs. F. M. Gray,	3.00 .... 16 ..
"	Ryan's,	James W. Ryan,	....
Covington,	Cox,	Dr. Carey Cox,	....
Dawson,	Dawson,	B. F. Collins,	2.50 A 10 ..
Ft. Gaines,	Central,	R. B. Peterson,	2.00 .... 10 ..
Ft. Valley,	Byington's	Byington & Wheeler	3.00 A ....
Gainesville,	Trammell's,	J.G.Trammell&Son	....
Greensboro,	Greensboro,	J. J. Dougherty,	....
Griffin,	Byington's,	G. W. Byington,	3.00 AM 15 ..
Homersville,	Crum's,	R. B. Crum,	2.00 AI ....
Jessup,	Jessup,	T. P. Littlefield,	2.00 AH 8 ..
"	Metropolitan,	A. M. Hayward,	3.00 AM 10 ..
La Grange,	McGee's,	T. W. McGee,	....
Macon,	Brown's,	E. E. Brown&Son,	3.00 ....
"	Lanier,	B. Dub,	....
"	National,	McBurney & Hollingsworth,	2.50 AI I 20
"	Planters,	I. H. Bremer	2.00 AF 8 14
Marietta,	Kennesaw,	J. Q. A. Lewis,	3.00 A ....
Millen,	Millen,	James M. Daniels,	....
Milledgeville,	McComb's,	M.H.&T.L.M'Comb	....
Norcross,	Norcross,	John J. Thrasher,	....
Quitman,	McIntosh,	Mrs. A. P. Perham,	2.00 AI 7 ..
Rome,	Choice,	J. C. Rawlins,	2.00 AI I ..
"	Stansbury's,	J. A. Stansbury,	....
Savannah.			
156 Bryan,	Bresnan's,	MauriceL.Harnett,	2.00 AI H ..
"	"	"	1.00 EF ....
176 St. Julien,	Girard,	Reeve & Girard,	....
Brighton near Drayton,	Marshall,	A. B. Luce,	3.00 ....
116 Bryan,	McConnell's,	A. Fernandez,	2.00 A 10 ..
Barn'd&Bryan,	Planters'	A. E. Carr,	2.50 AJ 10 ..
....	Pulaski,	S. N. Papot & Co.,	....
Bull&Congress,	Screven,	R. Bradley,	4.00 AS ....
StoneMountain,	Robert's,	E. A. Roberts,	....
St. Marys,	Spencer,	W. E. Stockwell,	3.00 A ....
Thomasville,	Gulf Railroad,	Geo. W. Parnell,	....
Valdosta,	Stuart'sRailr'd,	C. T. Stewart,	2.50 AK K 18

FLORIDA.

TOWN.	HOTEL.	PROPRIETOR.			
Baldwin,	Farmer's	G. W Ford,	2.50	AI	I ..
Cedar Keys,	Exchange	E. J. Shemwell,	2.50	AK	K ..
Fernandina,	Riddell	Samuel T. Riddell,	3.00	AN	12 ..
Green Cove Sp.,	Union	Bodine&McCarty,	4.00	AR	R ..
Jacksonville,	Metropolitan	A. C. Barnett,	3.00	AN	.. ..
"	Nicholl's	W. M. Nicholls,			
"	St. James	J. R. Campbell,	4.00		
"	Windsor	Scott & Moore,			
Key West,	Parker's	Parker&Sedwitch,			
Lake City,	Monroe				
"	Tresvant				
Melonville,	Melonville	E. S. White,	3.00	AM	15 25
Orlando,	Orlando	J. Summerlin,	2.25	AI	I ..
Palatka,	Putnam	F. H. Orvis,	4.00	AQ	25 ..
"	St. Johns	P. & H. Peterman,	3.00	AO	O ..
Pensacola,	Continental	Sinks & Palmer,	4.00	x	.. ..
"	Powell	J. V. Powell,	2.00	AJ	I 15
"	Santa Rosa	Mrs.J.C.Ackerman,			
Quincy,	Quincy	Mrs. J. S. Gibson,	2.50	AI	I 18
Sanford,	Sanford	J. B. Wistar,			
St. Augustine,	Magnolia,	W. W. Palmer,			
"	Oriental	W. G. Ponce & Co.	3.00	AK	K ..

ALABAMA.

TOWN.	HOTEL.	PROPRIETOR.			
Athens,	Leslie	William Leslie,			
Birmingham,	Ketchum's	Wm. Ketchum,			
Calera,	Welch's	Welch & Bro.,			
Clayton,	Sutlive's	J. W. Sutlive & Co.			
Courtland,	Parshall's	S. Parshall,			
Decatur,	Derrick's	L. W. Derrick,	1.50	AC	A ..
Demopolis,	City	John McClelland,	2.50	AI	I ..
Eufala,	Commercial	A. J. Riddle,	3.00	AM	15 24
"	Market,	A. A. Raleigh,			
Florence,	National	Anderson&White,	2.00	....	9 ..
Greenboro,	Johnson'	A. Johnson,	2.00	AI	J 18
Greenville,	City	J. A. Rhodes,	2.50	AI	I 15
Guntersville,	Greenwood's	G. Greenwood,	2.00	AG	G 15
Huntsville,	Easley's	Mrs. M. A. Easley,'			
"	Huntsville	C. S. Munson,	2.50	AK	K ..
La Fayette,	Marable's	Mrs.M.J.Marable,			
Marion,	King	J. D. Wellborn,	2.00	AI	J 20

ALABAMA.

TOWN.	HOTEL.	PROPRIETOR.		
Mobile.				
Royal and St. Francis St.,	Battle,	F. L. McGowan,	3.00 AR	....
31 Conti,	Campbell	Jas. W. Campbell,	......	....
123 Dauphin,	Girard	Mrs. E. Goldsmith,	......	....
S. E. Corner Conti & Water,	Gulf City,	Geo. W. Young,	......	....
32 N. Royal,	Smith&Dumas'	Smith & Dumas,	1.00 EG	....
Montgomery,	Central	S. Corzelins,	2.00 x	....
"	Exchange	Watt & Lanier,	3.00 AN	....
"	Madison	J. W. Baylis,	2.50 x	....
"	Merchants	S. Oppenheimer,	......	....
Opelika,	Adams'	Mrs. S. E. Adams & Son,	......	....
"	Bedell,	Frank A. Hervey	2.00 AJ	10 ..
Pollard,	Pollard	T. D. Wolfe,	......	....
Randolph,	Honeycutt's	Mrs.C.V.Honeycutt	2.00 AJ I	..
Tuscaloosa,	Broadway	Mrs.IsabellaLynch	2.00 AI J	20
Tuskegee,	Tuskegee	P. R. McKensie,	2.00 AJ I	..
Union Springs,	Pullam's	Thomas Pullam,	......	....

MISSISSIPPI.

TOWN.	HOTEL.	PROPRIETOR.		
Aberdeen,	Johnson's	I. Y. Johnson,	......	....
Artesia,	Artesia	W. P. Smith,	......	....
Baldwyn,	Forest	D. C. Williams,	2.00 A	11 ..
Brookhaven,	Maxwell's	Mrs.A.E.Maxwell,	......	....
Burnsville,	Baker's	Mrs.M.A.Sheehan,	2.00 A	10 ..
Canton,	Wolf's	Turk & Yeargain,	3.00 AM M	..
Columbus,	Gilmer	A. W. King,	3.00 AK	14 ..
Corinth,	Central	J. H. Morlan,	2.00 AF E	..
"	Hill's	H. F. Hill & Co.,	......	....
Crawford,	Exchange	James Nonce,	2.00 A	5 ..
Enterprise,	European	Fred'k Heims,	2.50 AI	5 ..
Grenada,	Chamberlain's	W.C.Chamberlain,	......	....
Hazelhurst,	Catchings'	T. J. Catchings,	......	....
Jackson,	Nelson	John Nelson,	2.50 AJ J	22
Macon,	Howell's	B. F. Howell,	2.50 AI I	18
Meridian,	Jones'	Josiah Jones,	1.00 AH D	..
MississippiCity	Mayer's	John D.Mayer&Co.	......	....
Muldon,	Manahan's	E. D. Manahan,	2.00 AH H	..

MISSISSIPPI.

TOWN.	HOTEL.	PROPRIETOR.			
Natchez,	Curry's	Mrs. Curry,			
"	**Jefferson**	S. W. Stockwell,	2.00 A I	I	17
"	Miller	Mrs. Hoebne,			
Okolona,	Foster's	Mrs. Emily Foster,			
Rienzi,	Whiteside	J. N. Whiteside,	2.00 A I	8	..
Shubuta,	Collins'	Robert Collins,	2.00 A F	D	..
State Line,	Moore's	Dr. M. Moore,	2.00 A I	7	14
Summit,	Dickey's	R. B. Dickey,			
Tupelo,	McPherson's	W. W. McPherson,			
Vicksburg,	La Madrid	Mme. La Madrid,	3.00 A P		
"	Prentiss	L. England,	2.50		14 ..
"	Washington	W. S. Lum,			
Winona,	Morin's	A. Morin,			
Woodville,	Kothe's	Mrs. Betty Kothie,			
Yazoo City,	Mound St,	Kent & Kline,			

LOUISIANA.

TOWN.	HOTEL.	PROPRIETOR.			
Alexandria,	Exchange	T. Hockstein	2.00 A I	I	..
Baton Rouge,	Hamey	Henry Gissell,			
"	Verandah	C. Cremonini,			
Carrollton,	Hickok's	D. S. Hickok,			
Clinton,	Worms'	Mrs. A. Worms,			
Donaldsonville,	Club House	P. Lefevre,			
Franklin,	**O'Neill's**	J. A. O'Neill,	2,50 A L	L	..
Houma,	Berger's	Peter Berger,			
Jackson,	Powers	J. Powers,			
Minden,	Reynolds'	A. J. Reynolds,	2.00 A	7	..
Monroe,	Lewis'	Mrs. M. J. Lewis,	2.50 A L	K	20
New Iberia,	Live Oak	Fitzhugh&Hilliard	2.00 A E	E	15
New Orleans.					
170 Gravier St.,	Cassidy's	Mrs.Marg. Cassidy	2.50 A		..
"	' "	" "	1.00 E		..
Camp and Common	City	Watson&Mumford,			
Girod and St. Peters,	Commercial	Conrad Miller,			
23 Conti,	Conti Veranda	Fred. Bayha,			
133 Chartres,	Old Orleans	F. Lasbennes,			
St. Charles St.,	St. Charles	Rivers Lonsdale & Co.,	4.50		..
....	St. James	R. E. Rivers & Co.,			
N. Peters,	Texas	StephenM.Terrell,			
101 Camp,	Waverly	ThomasW.Kidder	2.00		10 ..

LOUISIANA.

TOWN.	HOTEL.	PROPRIETOR.		
Opelousas,	Eureka	A. Lacombe,	2.00 AI	I '..
Shreveport,	Dreyfus'	C. & W. Dreyfus,		
Tangipahoe,	Daniels'	Wm. J. Daniels,		
Thibodeaux,	Albert's	Mrs. Thos. Albert,		
Vermillionville,	Smith's	Mrs.Wm.O. Smith,		
Washington,	Trainor's	Francis Trainor		

TEXAS.

TOWN.	HOTEL.	PROPRIETOR.			
Austin,	Avenue	T. J. Moore,	3.00 AL	L	..
"	Raymond	John H. Sterett,	3.00 AN	O	..
Bastrop,	Nicholson's	James Nicholson,	2.00 AG	G	16
Brenham,	Peabody	James E. Slater,	2.00 AE	D	..
Bremond,	Bremond	Mrs. N.W.Brooks,	2.00 AJ	5	..
Bryan,	Barnett's	E. D. Barnett,			
Columbus,	**Wootton**	J. B. Knotts,	2.50 AL	14	..
Corsicana,	Molloy's	Hugh L. Malloy,			
Crockett,	Hall's	W. E. Hall,	2.00 A	9	..
Dallas,	Commercial,	Root & Crozier,			
"	Rawlins'	E. R. Rawlins,			
Denison	Fuller's	E. E. Fuller,			

Galveston.

Mechanic & Tremont St.,	Cosmopolitan	J. B. Biron & Co.,		
19th & Ave. H.,	Exchange	Mrs. S. B. White		
24th & Market,	Girardin	Romanent & Girardin,	3.00 AN	N ..
Mechanic & 22d,	GrandSouthern	Sbisa & Orfila,		
Centre&Church	Patrick	E. H. Patrick,	2.00 AF	F 17
Market & 26th,	Planters	M. K. Strickland,	2.00	10 ..
Centre & Mechanic,	Washington	John Summers,	2.50 AL	L ..
Tremont Ave.,	Waters	E. R. Nichols		
Hallville,	Holland's	N. Holland,		
Hearne,	Downing's	S. Downing,		
Hempstead,	City	Jones & Sloan,		
Houston,	Dissen's	Wm. Dissen,	2.50 AL	10 ..
"	Exchange	Daniel S. Sargent,	2.50 AM	L ..
"	Hutchings	Harrell & Harbeck,		
"	Tremont	A. Sens,	1.50 AE	E ..
Jefferson,	Central	Johnson & Busser,		
Marlin,	Nicholson's	W.A.J. Nicholson,		

TEXAS.

TOWN.	HOTEL.	PROPRIETOR.				
Marshall,	Capitol	W. H. Whitla,	3.00	A M		
"	King	E. A. Mahaffey,				
"	Texas & Pacific,	L.H.Norwood&Co.				
McKinney,	McKinney	James McKinney,				
Mexia,	Gatlin	W. L. Beckham,	2.00	A I	J	
Navasota,	Freeman's	J.H.Freeman&Co.				
New Braunfels,	Lyon's	T. L. Lyon,				
Paris,	McLeod's	J. B. McLeod,	3.00		21	
Rusk,	Taylor	Harrison C. Stout,				
San Antonio,	Menger's	Mrs.W.A.Menger,	2.50	A K	16	30
Sherman,	Southern	Thomas Smith,				
Tyler,	City	J. W. Wooton,	1.50	A F	F	15
Waco	Kirkpatrick's	Mrs. M. H. Kirkpatrick,				

KENTUCKY.

TOWN.	HOTEL.	PROPRIETOR.				
Auburn,	Crewsdon's	W. N. Crewsdon,				
Bardstown,	Ellis'	Benj. Ellis & Son,				
Bowling Green,	Ritter's	Mrs. M. A. Ritter,				
Columbus,	Jackson's	J. M. Jackson,				
Covington,	Central	John Sommers,	2.00		10	
"	Rothert's	Frank Rothert,				
Crab Orchard,	Harris'	M. S. Harris,				
Cynthiana,	Nebel's	H. C. Nebel,				
Danville,	Fields'	Wm. M. Fields,				
Eddyville,	Brasswell's	N. T. Brasswell,				
Elizabethtown,	Slack's	James B. S. Slack,				
Falmouth,	Jefferson	G. C. Lightfoot,	2.00	A I		
Frankfort,	Frankfort	D. Merriweather,				
"	Weitzel's	Jerome Weitzel,				
Franklin,	Boisseau	R. T. Bryant,	2.00	A I	10	
Greenville,	Reno's	L. R. Reno,	2.00	A I	J	20
Harrodsburg,	Hoffman's	J. J. Hoffman,				
Hartford,	Vaught's	J. S. Vaught,	1.50	A A	A	9
Henderson,	Audubon,	Mrs. Robt. Evans,	1.25	A D	D	13
"	Hord's	Frank P. Hord,	2.50		14	
Hickman,	St. Charles	Emile Scharfe,	2.00	A I	10	
Hopkinsville,	Millen's	M. G. Millen,				
La Grange,	Bain's	T. J. Bain,				
"	Kenyon's	Mrs. John Kenyon,				
Lebanon,	Harris'	R. C. Harris,				

TOWN.	HOTEL.	PROPRIETOR.		
Lexington,	Carson's	R. Carson,	2.00	9 ..
"	St. Nicholas	J. W. Stockton,	2.50 AI	14 ..

Louisville.

84 Main St.,	Alexander's	J.B.Alexander&Co.	2.00	10 ..
7th & Market,	Central	Stamp & Wheeler,	2.00	10 ..
Main & 1st,	Galt	J. P. Johnson,	....	..
Main near 6th,	Louisville,	M. Kean & Co.,	....	..
60 Market,	Market	Mrs.Wm. Knoller,	....	..
6th near Main,	Merchants	Ray & Evans,	2.00 AJ	J 20
9th & B'dway,	New Era	D. S. Martin,	....	..
7th & Main,	St. Charles	F. Hartman,	....	..
2d & Jefferson,	St. Cloud	Phil Peters,	2.50 AJ	J 22
6th & Court Pl.	St. Nicholas	Weilage & Seekamp,	1.50 EJ	.. ..
Shelby & Main,	Shelby	George Birch,	....	..
....	Southern	Dr. J. A. Hoke,	....	..
125 First,	Spencer	Staple & Mechornay,	....	..,
....	Wolf's	Joseph Wolf,	....	..,
Maysville,	Patterson's	S. B. Patterson,	2.00 AI	I ..
Midway,	Thornton's	Mrs. Thornton,	....	..
Millersburg,	Purnell's	W. T. Purnell,	....	..
Millwood,	Wells'	H. R. Wells,	2.00 AF	E 12
Mt. Sterling,	Central	W.S. & J.Thomas,	....	..
Nicholasville,	Sparks'	Dr. J. S Sparks	....	..
Owensboro,	Wickliffe's	Wickliffe Bros.,	....	..
Paducah,	Ross'	Mrs. E. A. G. Ross,	....	..
Paris,	Bourbon	D. Turney,	3.00	14 ..
"	Thurston	John Griffith,	2.50 AI	I ..
Richmond,	Ballard's	Ballard Wilkerson & Co.,	....	..
Rockport,	Moore's	E. G. Moore,	....	..
Russellville,	Forest	Roberts&Bowling,	2.00 AJ	10 ..
"	Gray's	S. B. Ryan,	2.00 AI	I ..
Shelbyville,	Armstrong's	Geo.A.Armstrong,	....	..
Versailles,	Versailles	W. J. Stitt,	2.00 AJ	10 ..
Walton,	Boone	John G. Snow,	1.50 AF	F ..
Winchester,	Hayes'	Stephen Hayes,	....	..,

TENNESSEE.

TOWN.	HOTEL.	PROPRIETOR.			
Bristol,	Thomas'	J. M. Thomas,	...		
Brownsville,	New Exchange	Henderson & Tracy,	3.00	AJ	11 20
Chattanooga,	Commercial	J. W. F. Bryson,	2.00	...	11 ..
"	Van Horn	M. D. Van Horn,	3.00	AL	...
Clarkesville,	Scott's	T. D. Scott,	...		
Cleveland,	Delano	S. H. De Armond,	2.00	AI	I ..
Columbia,	Guest's	James L. Guest,	2.00	AI	7 ..
Franklin,	Parish's	H. D. Parish,	...		
Greenville,	Godfrey's	Wm. A. Godfrey,	2.00	AE	D ..
Humboldt,	Humboldt	Coleman & Perry,	...		
Huntingdon,	Brower's	R. T. Brower,	1.25	AF	6 ..
"	Johnson's	R. J. Johnson,	2.00	AH	6 ..
Huntsville,	Sharp's	Wm. Sharp,	1.00	AA	A ..
Jackson,	Commercial	Wm. G. Smith,	2.50	AI	I 18
Jonesboro,	Sevier's	James Sevier,	...		
Kenton,	West's	J. R. West,	...		
Knoxville,	Sheriff's	John Sheriff,	...		
Lebanon,	Hardy's	Mrs. J. W. Hardy,	2.00	...	5 ..
Marysville,	McKenzie's	R. McKenzie,	...		
McMinnville,	Mason's	R. H. Mason,	...		
Memphis.					
Adams near 2d St.	Central	C. F. Jackson,	...		
Jefferson & Front,	Commercial	Hastings & Landis,	...		
Ayres Block 2d St.	European	M. F. Ball,	...		
118 Adams,	Franklin	F. Ruser,	1.50	...	8 ..
Front & Market,	Freeman's	C. P. Freeman,	1.00	AA	A ..
351 Front,	Green Tree	John Ringwald,	1.50	AF	E ..
Main & Monroe,	Peabody	O. Bannion & Morris,	4.00	...	
109 Adams,	Whitmore	Mrs. Smith,	...		
Main & Adams,	Worsham	White & Jones,	...		
Morristown,	Cain's	T. C. Cain,	...		
Murfreesboro,	City	Jones & Roe,	...		
Nashville.					
123 Church St.,	Battle	Crockett & Ransom,	...		
Deaderick St.,	City	J. A. Holt & Co.,	...		
Cedar St.,	Commercial	J. G. Fulgham,	...		
Walnut & Church,	Depot	J. A. Kellogg,	1.50	AH	G 14
51 S. Market,	Dix's	John H. Dix,	1.50	AF	7 ..

TENNESSEE.

Nashville.	HOTEL.	PROPRIETOR.	
103 N. College,	Franklin	E. Franklin,	....
Cherry near Church,	Maxwell	J. H. Fulton & Co.	....
Spruce near Cherry,	Nicholson	J. C. Nicholson,	2.00 ....
35 N. Market,	St. Charles	J. M. Armstrong,	2.00 AH H ..
Paris,	Paris	D. J. Alexander,	2.00 A 10 ..
Pulaski,	Alamo	A. E. Fuller,	2.50 .... 11 ..
Shelbyville,	Evans	Greer & Co.,	2.00 AI I ..
"	Grange	Mrs. A. M. Ross,	1.50 ....
Somerville,	Cabler's	L. F. Cabler,	....
"	Wetherby's	Wm. Wetherby,	....
Troy,	Anderson's	Mary Anderson,	....

ARKANSAS.

TOWN.	HOTEL.	PROPRIETOR.	
Arkadelphia,	Ray's,	John C. Ray,	....
Augusta,	Woodruff,	James L. Barnes,	2.00 .... 10 ..
Bentonville,	Clark's,	J. W. Clark,	.75 .... 4 ..
Clarksville,	Clarksville,	F. M. Paine,	1.50 AE 7 ..
Fort Smith,	St. Charles,	Ed. H. Fleming,	2.00 .... 7 ..
Helena,	Shelby,	Mrs. J. Wayne,	3.00 AM L ..
Hot Springs,	Buchanan's,	F.C.Buchanan&Co.	... .
"	Hot Springs,	L. Kraus & Co.,	2.50 ....
Little Rock,	Arkansas,	G. Ehmann,	....
"	Central,	Mrs. A. Mimrick,	2.00 AI I ..
"	Metropolitan,	A. G. De Shon,	1.00 EG .. ..
"	Virginia,	Mrs. W. R. Rock,	....
Napoleon,	Gilroy's,	P. M. Gilroy,	....
Pine Bluff,	McKenney,	W. J. McKenney,	2.00 AG H ..
Princeton,	Holmes,	Mrs. M. A. Holmes,	... .
Searcy,	Kellum's,	James P. Kellum,	....
Van Buren,	Planters',	James Brodie,	1.50 AF E ..
Waldron,	Waldron,	F. Malone,	1.50 AG G ..
Washington,	Winn's,	Daniel R. Winn,	....

82   OHIO.

TOWN.	HOTEL.	PROPRIETOR.			
Ada,	Ada,	Lydia A. Warner,	1.00	....	4 ..
Akron,	Buckeye,	S. O. Raber,	1.50	AD D	..
"	City,	Fred. Hedeman,	2.00	AD D	..
"	Empire,	R. N. Downey,	...	...	.. ..
Alliance,	Genter's,	John Genter,	...	...	.. ..
"	Sourbeck's,	Dan'l Sourbeck,	...	...	.. ..
Andover,	Keene's,	W. J. Keen,	...	...	.. ..
Antwerpt,	Ellsworth's,	A. Ellsworth,	...	...	.. ..
Ashland,	McNulty's,	Wm. McNulty,	...	...	.. ..
"	Miller's,	MICHAEL MILLER,	2.00	AI	I 18
Ashtabula,	Booth's,	Thomas N. Booth,	...	...	.. ..
Athens,	Cornell's,	F. Cornell & Son,	...	...	.. ..
"	Warren,	W. H. McMonigal,	2.00	....	10 ..
Attica,	Ayres',	David Ayres,	1.00	A	5 ..
Auburn,	Auburn,	C. A. Hunt,	1.00	A	5 ..
Austintown,	Corl's,	Eli Corl,	...	...	.. ..
Barnesville,	Frazier's,	R. E. Frazier,	...	...	.. ..
Bellefontaine,	Logan,	Wm. Keyes,	2.00	....	5 ..
"	Ward's,	J. W. Ward,	...	...	.. ..
Bellaire,	Morris',	E. C. Morris,	...	...	.. ..
Belleville,	Garn's,	A. Garn,	2.00	AI	I 15
Bellevue,	Exchange,	E. W. Dorsey,	...	...	.. ..
Berea,	Nichols',	John Nichols,	...	...	.. ..
Bluffton,	Dray's,	John R. Dray,	...	...	.. ..
Bowling Green,	American,	Hugh Carjo,	1.00	AB	7 ..
"	Ross',	J. H. Ross,	...	...	.. ..
Bryan,	Fountain City,	A. Gilbert,	2.00	AJ J	..
"	Exchange,	W. H. Sink,	2.00	A	.. ..
Bucyrus,	Sim's,	Capt.A.G.Thornton	2.00	AF	6 11
Bremen,	Wilson,	Margaret Smock,	1.00	AB	6 ..
Caldwell,	Perry's,	J. B. Perry & Son,	...	...	.. ..
Cambridge,	Brown's,	Mrs. N. Brown,	...	...	.. ..
"	New Eagle,	....	2.00	AI	J 18
Canal Dover,	Kings,	David King,	...	...	.. ..
Canal Fulton,	City,	Lewis Walser,	1.00	A	5 ..
Canfield,	Clark's,	Wm. H. Clark,	...	...	.. ..
Canton,	Ely's,	E. D. Ely,	...	...	.. ..
"	Ogden,	A. L. Rothacker,	2.00	....	14 ..
Chardon,	Benton's,	Benton & Co.,	...	...	.. ..
Chilicothe,	Emmitt,	L. A. Bowers,	2.50	....	.. ..
"	Hirn's,	Anthony Hirn,	...	...	.. ..
"	Warner's,	Jacob Warner,	2.50	....	14 ..
Circleville,	Pickaway,	C. D. French,	...	...	.. ..
"	American,	P. W. Rodgers,	2.00	....	.. ..

OHIO.

TOWN.	HOTEL.	PROPRIETOR.		
Cincinatti.				
203 Broadway,	Adams',	Solomon Adams,	1.50	7..
Main & 5th St.	Arlington	John W. Garrison & Co.		
Court & Walnut,	Bevis,	F. B. James,	1.50	8..
Vine & 3d-st.,	Burnet,	Dunkler, Sailer & Co.	4.00 AQ	
Walnut & 6th-st.,	Crawford,	Frank J. Oakes,	2.50	
Court & Race-st.,	Farmers',	Gus Schiller,	1.25 AC	C..
Main & 6th-st.,	**Galt,**	HUMMELL, AIR & CO.	2.00 AH F	17
40 West Court-st.	Germania,	Sebastian Peng,	1.25 A	5..
Walnut & 4th-st.,	New Gibson,	Geffroy & Gibson,	3.00	
Central-av & 4th,	Grand,	Gilmore & Sons,	4.00	
Wood & 5th-st.,	Great Western,	Anton Hoess,	1.50 AF D	..
3d-st., n'r Main,	Henrie,	James Watson,	.:	
Vine-st., n'r 5th,	Hunt's,	C. B. Hunt & Co.,		
163 W. 5th-st.,	Indiana,	G. Ryman,	1.50 AF	
Main, n'r Front,	Madison,	John W. Garrison,	2.25 AF	10..
421 Main,	Mansion	Ernst Hesse,	150 AF D	..
5th, n'r Syracuse,	Merchants',	Henry E. Carter,		
Sycamore & 9th,	Miller,	J. S. Goldtrap & Co.,	1.25 AF	7..
9th & Vine,	Pfeiffer's,	Mrs. C. Pfeiffer,		
175 Sycamore,	Rowe,	J. Faulkner & Son,	1.25	5..
4th, n'r Main,	St. James,	J. J. McGrath,		
4th & Race,	St. Nicholas,	B. Roth & Sons,	2.00 E	..
15 East 9th,	Teutonia,	Wenzel Beinl,	1.25 A	7..
Walnut, n'r 7th,	Walnut Street,	F. Y. Batchelor & Co.	2.50	14..
3d & Broadway,	Winnie,	John B. Lucas,	1.25 A	7..
Cleveland.				
134 Superior	American,	A. Jones,	2.50	
122 Water,	Burch,	L. D. Hunt,	2.00	10..
Seneca & Rockwell,	City,	James Current,	2.00	11..
Seneca & Champlin,	Clinton,	Hawley & Langton,	1.50 AF E	..
Public Square & Superior,	Forest City,	Terrill & Ingersoll,	3.00 AK	..
185 Pearl,	Franklin,	W. B. Gilbert,	1.50 AE D	..
32 Bank,	**Lake Shore,**	J. DUNN,	1.50 AH E	..
Pearl & Willey,	Pearl Street,	Henry & Gray,	1.00 AA A	..
Superior & Bank,	Weddell,	G. W. Wesley & Son,	3.00	21..
Clyde,	Pierce's,	Mary L. Pierce,		
Columbus.				
State & High,	American,	E. J. Blount,	2.50 AL	..
Broad, near Washington,	Broadway,	Stephen Hicks,	1.50	5..

OHIO.

Columbus.	HOTEL.	PROPRIETOR.	
156 N. High,	City,	G. J. Scarbrough,	....
High&Naghton	Davidson's,	J. H. Davidson,	.75 ED ....
176 N. High,	Empire,	James Johnson,	....
273 N. High,	Exchange,	H. Kauffman,	....
High, n'r State,	Neil House,	Walstein Failing,	3.00 AM ....
High & Fulton,	Parr,	Samuel Older,	....
141 E. Town,	Town Street,	J. Chamberlin,	1.25 AC 7 ..
73 W. Broad,	West Broad St.,	J. Marquart & Bro.,	1.50 AE E 15
4th & Friend,	Zettler,	L. S. Upton,	1.50 AF F 16
ColumbusGrove	Grove,	John B. Fruckey,	1.50 AF A 8
Conneaut,	Commercial,	Miles Doman,	2.00 .... 8 ..
Coshocton,	Price's,	W. H. H. Price,	2.00 AI I ..
"	City,	John H. Lowrie,	....
Crestline,	Russell's,	L. G. Russell & Co.,	....
Cuyahoga Falls,	Perry's,	John F. Perry & Son,	2.00 A 7 ..

Dayton.

3d, n'r Jefferson,	**Beckel,**	LOUIS REIBOLD,	3.50 AP N ..
34 W. 6th,	Buckeye,	James Ward,	1.50 .... 7 ..
6th, n'r Main,	City,	John B. Kruse,	1.50 .... 7 ..
3d, n'r Madison,	Dayton,	James Nugent,	....
6th & Ludlow,	Dickey,	Geo. W. Mesler,	1.50 .... 9 ..
24 E. 2d,	Knecht's,	Christ Knecht,	....
24 Market,	Liberty Hall,	Mrs. Geo. Herbig,	1.50 AC A ...
2d, n'r Main,	**Merchants,**	A. L. Ross, Jr.,	2.00 AI ....
3d, n'r Canal,	Park,	Wm. Rufaber,	2.00 AH F ..
Main, n'r 6th,	Phenix,	Greble Harvey,	....
126 E. 3d,	Sanders',	Wm. Sanders,	....
129 E. 2d,	Schieble's,	B. Schieble,	2.00 AJ J ..
Defiance,	Blanchard's,	Joseph Blanchard,	....
"	Heacock's,	Larkin Heacock,	....
Delaware,	American,	Joseph Johnson,	....
Delphos,	Brown's,	N. H. Webb,	2.00 ....
Delta,	Crosby's,	O. V. Crosby,	....
Dresden,	St. Charles	Peter R. Swope,	....
Dunkirk,	American,	H. N. Hullinger,	....
East Liverpool,	City,	M. Hilbert,	2.00 AI G 15
Eaton,	Deem's,	John T. Deem,	....
Elmore,	Rice's,	R. Rice,	....
Elyria,	Bliss',	Zenas Bliss,	....
"	Hall's,	Edwin Hall,	....
Enorn,	Enorn,	P. J. Brewer,	1.50 AC C ..
Findlay,	Joy's,	A. & D. Joy,	....

OHIO. 85

TOWN.	HOTEL.	PROPRIETOR.	
Fostoria,	American,	Charles J. Myers,	1.00 A A A ..
"	Reed's,	W. W. Reed,	... ...
Frankfort,	Miller's,	Isaac Miller,	... ...
Franklin,	Miller's,	Casper Miller,	... ...
Fredericktown,	Wagner's,	Chas. Wagner,	... ...
Fremont,	Ford's,	John Ford,	... ...
Galion,	Pratt's,	C. E. Pratt,	... ...
Gallipolis,	Dunn's,	John Dunn,	... ...
"	Merchant's,	H. Lautenschlaeger	1.00 A A A ..
Garrettsville,	Nye & Smith's,	Nye & Smith,	... ...
Germantown,	Leighty's,	Wm. Leighty,	... ...
Grafton,	Smith's,	A. D. Smith,	... ...
Granville,	Buxton's,	M. H, Buxton,	... ...
Green Springs,	Green Spring,	E. B. Finch,	2.00 .... 10 ..
Greenville,	Turpen's,	T. P. Turpen&Son,	2.00 A I I 18
Groveport,	Campbell's,	Chas. Campbell,	... ...
Hamden,	American,	McClure & Curry,	2.00 A I I ..
Hamilton,	Galt,	F. B. Martin,	... ...
"	Philipps',	A. A. Philipps,	... ...
"	St. Julien,	Wm. Gundrum,	... ...
"	Straub,	W. A. Cox,	2.00 A I G 14
Harrison,	Mead's,	Wm. Mead,	... ...
Hillsboro,	Cook's,	A. T. Cook,	... ...
Hubbard,	Lynn's,	C. Lynn,	... ...
Hudson,	Mansion,	Chas. Banton,	... ...
Ironton,	Wood's,	Oliver Wood & Son,	... ...
Jackson,	Gibson's,	Levi B. Gibson,	... ...
Jefferson,	Baldwin's,	J. H. Baldwin,	... ...
Kent,	Burger,	W. C. Burger,	... ...
Kenton,	Reese's,	Henry Reese,	... ...
Lancaster,	American,	Chas. F. Bowman,	... ...
"	Mitthoff,	C. Davis,	2.00 x .. ..
"	Wetzel,	J. Wetzel,	... ...
Lebanon,	Lebanon,	W. G. Smith,	... ...
Leesburg,	Griffith's,	John Griffith,	... ...
Leetonia,	Leetonia,	Samuel Duck,	2.00 A H D 12
"	Meek's,	Joseph Meek,	... ...
Lima,	Brownell's,	E. Brownell,	... ...
"	Lima,	J. Goldsmith,	2.00 ....
Logan,	Rempel,	W. H. Ambrose,	2.00 .... 5 ..
London,	Madison,	A. Dunkin,	2.00 A H G ..
Londonville,	American,	John Stockman,	... ...
Louisville,	Moinett's,	Julian Moinetts,	... ...

OHIO.

TOWN.	HOTEL.	PROPRIETOR.			
Lynchburg,	Miller's,	W. C. Miller,	...		
Madison,	Judd's,	Z. L. Judd,	...		
Manchester,	St. Charles,	David Charles,	1.50	AH	6 ..
Mansfield,	Sherman,	Suman & Keister,	...		
"	St. James,	Van Hoff & Bird,	...		
"	Townley's,	C. C. Townley,	...		
"	Wiler,	Field & Myers,	...		
Marietta,	Commercial,	John L. Barbour,	2.00	AF	F ..
"	National,	T. R. Wells,	2.00	x	.. ..
Marion,	Exchange,	H. C. Eppley,	1.50	AF	D ..
"	Cochran's,	J. M. Cochran,	...		
Marysville,	St. Clair,	Will S. Smith,	2.00	AJ	7 11
Massillon,	American,	M. Madison,	2.00	AI	J 20
"	Tremont,	F. H. Killinger,	2.00	AI	J ..
Maumee City,	White's,	David White,	...		
McArthur,	Redd's,	Horace Redd,	...		
McConnellsville	Adam's,	Jacob Adams,	...		
Miamisburg,	Weaver's,	Henry Weaver,	...		
Middletown,	Furry's,	Mrs. R. Furray,	...		
Millersburg,	Butler's,	Joseph Butler,	2.00	AG	G 16
Minerva,	Centre,	Jacob Unger,	1.00	....	4 ..
"	Hewett's,	J. D. Hewett,	...		
Morrow,	Miami,	E. W. Newlove,	2.00	AH	9 ..
"	Ready's,	B. T. Ready,	...		
Monroeville,	Bergin's,	George D. Bergin,	2.00	....	5 ..
Mt. Vernon,	Rowley's,	H. Y. Rowley,	2.00	AI	I ..
"	Commercial,	F. McBride & Son,	...		
Napoleon,	Hotchkiss,	C. A. Hotchkiss,	...		
"	Vocke,	A. Gilbert,	2.00	AI	.. ..
Nelsonville,	Meyers',	H. H. Myers,	1.50	AH	7 12
Newark,	Giraeffe,	Mrs. Young,	1.00	AA	A ..
"	Lansing's,	Robert Lansing,	2.00	x	.. ..
" ,	Park,	Peter Miller,	2.00	x	.. ..
"	Penn,	J. W. Jordan,	...		
Newburg,	Spencer's,	A. J. Spencer,	...		
New Bremen,	Henke's,	H. Henke,	...		
New Lexington,	Central,	T. O'Brian,	...		
"	Neal,	J. F. Wilkers,	2.00	AI	J 20
New Lisbon,	Cowan's,	A. J. Cowan,	...		
New London,	Gregory,	Gregory & Van Horn	2.00	AI	I ..
New Phil'delph'a	Exchange,	C. B. Harvey,	2.00	....	5 ..
New Richmond,	Carey's,	F. N. Carey,	...		
Niles,	Niles,	Sanford & Pearce,	...		
Nor'h Lewisbu'g	Partridge's,	H. C. Partridge,	2.00	AI	9 ..

TOWN.	HOTEL.	PROPRIETOR.			
Norwalk,	St. Charles,	Chas. H. Botsford,	2,00	AI	I ..
Oberlin,	Field's,	Henry F. Field,	...	...	.. ..
Orrville,	Mansion,	Samuel Fasig,	1.50	AE	E 12
Orrwell,	Stone's,	R. E. Stone,	...	...	.. ..
Ottawa,	Row's,	Michael Row,	...	...	.. ..
Painesville,	Planters',	Frank O'Brien,	1.50	AA	A 10
"	Stockwell,	Henry Field,	2.00	AI	J ..
Paulding,	Furgison's,	J. A. Furgison,	...	...	.. ..
Perrysburg,	Norton's,	C. W. Norton,	...	...	.. ..
Piqua,	City,	H. Clay Worley,	...	...	.. ..
"	Leland,	Geo. H. Stayman,	...	...	.. ..
Plymouth,	Connell's,	Geo. Connell,	...	...	.. ..
Pomeroy,	Gibson,	George Todd,	2.00	....	7 ..
Portsmouth,	Biggs',	Pendergrast & Jennings,	2.50	AK	L ..
"	Degler's,	Fred. Degler,	...	...	.. ..
"	Central,	Reminger & Son,	...	...	.. ..
"	Massie,	E. Todd,	...	...	.. ..
Put-In-Bay,	Beebe's,	Beebe & Bro.,	...	...	.. ..
"	Put-In-Bay,	Sweney, West&Co.,	...	...	.. ..
Ravenna,	Ward's,	Lyman L. Ward,	...	...	.. ..
Ripley,	Bank,	....	2.00	AI	7 14
Sabina,	Rapp's,	Joseph Rapp,	...	...	.. ..
Salem,	Dellenbaugh's,	J. A. Dellenbaugh,	...	...	.. ..
Salineville,	McPherson's,	Eliz'beth M'Pherson	...	...	.. ..
Sandusky,	American,	J. Scott & Son,	1.50	AF	A ..
"	Colton,	Henry Colton,	...	...	.. ..
"	Germania,	A. M. Schelb,	1.00	....	6 ..
"	West's,	West & Powers,	2.50	....	.. ..
Shelby,	Junction,	C. P. Nichols,	2.00	....	7 ..
Sidney,	Stewart's,	J. R. Stewart,	...	...	.. ..
Solon,	Rathburn's,	G. S. Rathburn,	...	...	.. ..
Springfield,	Lagonda,	G.S.Atkinson&Son,	2.50	....	.. ..
"	Murray,	W. Knaub,	...	...	.. ..
Steubenville,	Cochran Centr'l	Getsman & Strickmaker,	...	...	.. ..
"	United States,	J. R. Mosgrove,	2.00	....	.. ..
St. Clairsville,	Frasier's,	W. P. Frasier,	...	...	.. ..
St. Marys,	Barr's,	John H. Barr,	...	...	.. ..
Thurman,	Home,	Wm. L. Williams,	1.25	AD	4 ..
Tiffin,	Myer's,	Peter P. Myers,	...	...	.. ..
Tippecanoe,	Carl's,	D. Carls,	...	...	.. ..

OHIO.

TOWN.	HOTEL.	PROPRIETOR.			
Toledo.					
111 St. Clair-st.,	American,	Gaines & Hamlin,	2.00	AJ	.. ..
461 Summit,	Hurd,	S. G. Van Buren,	2.00	AF	10 ..
Perry&Summit,	Lake Shore,	J. Englehardt,	1.50	AD	7 ..
Broadway,	Oliver,	Donald McDonald,	2.50	AK K	..
1st & Oak,	Oregon,	C. F. Yeslin,	1.50	AB	A ..
151 St. Clair,	Toledo,	John Mackin,	1.00	AA	A ..
Troy,	Hatfield,	J. W. Dutton,	2.00	AG	G 16
UpperSandusky	Hudson,	John W. Lime,	2.00	AF	E ..
Urichsville,	United States,	W. H. Dempster,	1.50	AH	7 12
Urbanna,	Exchange,	D. W. Sowles,	2.00		
"	Washington,	Charles McCarthy,			
"	Weaver,	N. Downing & Son,	2.00	AI	12 ..
Van Wert,	Van Wert,	C. Neff,	2.00	AI	7 ..
Vienna,	Vienna,	T. D. Mackey,			
Wapakonetta,	Burnett,	F. H. Kenthan,	2.00		
Warren,	National,	Phineas Chase,	2.00	AI	I ..
Warsaw,	Sherman,	Jas. M. Cochran,			
Washington,	Shaws',	Shaw & Shaw,	2.00	AI	I ..
Washingt'nville	Brady's,	John Brady,			
Wellington,	American,	S. E. Wilcox,			
Wellsville,	Cooper's,	Wm. Cooper,	1.00	AA	A ..
"	National,	Ernst Herwig,	1.50		6 ..
West Liberty,	Ginn's,	Benjamin Ginn,			
Willoughby,	Gildersleeve's,	S. D. Gildersleeve,			
"	Willoughby,	Mark Hammond,	1.00	AB	A ..
Wilmington,	Gates,	Wm. Thompson,			
Wooster,	American,	D. B. Ihrig,	2.50	AI	I ..
"	Washington,	E. B. Connelly,	1.75	AF	F ..
Xenia,	St. George,	George A. Bradley,			
"	Snell's,	R. F. Snell,			
Youngstown,	American,	Tom Thomas,	1.25		5 ..
"	Maitland's,	J. K. Maitland,			
Zanesville,	American,	William Getz,	2.00	AJ	I ..
"	Kirk's,	W. & S. M. Kirk,			
"	Mills',	J. C. Stevens,			
"	Roush,	Roush & Hatcher,			
"	Zane,	Mrs. A. E. Cook,			

TOWN.	HOTEL.	PROPRIETOR.			
Anderson,	Griffith's,	George R. Griffith,			
Angola,	Russell's,	P. W. Russell,	2.00	AH	6 ..
Antioch,	Mrs. Merkel's,	Mrs. M. C. Merkel,			
Argos,	Alleman's,	Wm. Alleman,			
Attica,	Revere,	John P. Gross,			
Auburn,	Swinford's,	S. C. Swinford,	2.00		
Aurora,	Hamiton's,	John Hamilton,			
Bedford,	Bedford,	Samuel Judah,	2.00	AHH	18
Bloomington,	Orchard's,	S.M.Orchard&Son,			
Bluffton,	Burgan's,	C. S. Burgan,	2.00	AI	8 ..
"	Exchange,	ThomasH.Gutelius	2.00	AI	I 15
Bourbon,	Bourbon,	Henry Sheets,	1.75	AH	6 10
Brazil,	National,	E. Ripley,	2.00		
Brookville,	**Valley,**	Peter Schaaf,	2.00	AI	5 10
Butler,	Moore's,	Samuel J. Moore,			
Cambridge City,	Vinton's,	Eldridge Vinton,			
Cannelton,	Scott's,	W. W. Scott,			
Centreville,	American,	Thos. S. Rowan,			
Charleston,	Liter's,	Capt. John Liter,	1.00	AA	A ..
Columbus,	Bowlin,	John A. Feiton,	2.00	AG	7 ..
Columbia City,	Rhodes',	John Rhodes, ●			
Connersville,	Avenue,	J. & R. Atwood,	2.00		7 ..
Crawfordsville,	Richardson's,	W. H. Springgate,	2.00	AI	10 ..
Crown Point,	Exchange,	Mrs.AngelineHack			
Decatur,	Burt's,	Chester Burt,			
Delphi,	Knight's,	C. M. Knight,			
Dillsboro,	Richt's,	Leonard Richt,			
Edwardsport,	Hinton's,	J. C. Hinton,	1.50	AE	A ..
Elkhart,	Clark's,	Henry Clark,			
Evansville,	Sherwood,	U. G. Damron,	2.00	AI	.. ..
"	St. George,	Mackey & Huston,	4.00	AM	.. ..
Fort Wayne,	Aveline's,	Mrs. Aveline,	3.00		
"	Exchange,	A. Freeman,	2.00	AF	E ..
"	Robinson,	J. H. Buckels,	2.00		
Franklin,	Strohman's,	Wm. Strohman,			
Frankfort,	Franklin's,	John Franklin,			
Fremont,	American,	Theron Storrs,			
Goshen,	Croxton's,	Capt. J. L. Croxton,			
Gosport,	Troth's,	H. J. Troth,			
Greencastle,	Jones',	J. F. Jones,			
Greenfield,	Nills',	M. T. Nills,			
Greensburg,	Seitz,	Chris Seitz,	2.00	AE	E ..
Hagerstown,	Clifton's,	M. F. Clifton,	2.00		7 ..

TOWN.	HOTEL.	PROPRIETOR.		
Hamilton,	Andrews',	H. N. Andrews,		
Hartford,	Edson's,	L. O. Edson,		
Huntington,	Holt's,	Mrs. E. N. Holt,		
Indianapolis.				
Illinois&Wash.	Hotel Bates,	Jas. O. Ives & Co.,	3.00	AN N
188 St. Albans,	California,	Mrs. C. Dornon,		
Missouri&Wash	Capitol,	M. K. Fatout,	2.00	11
Illinois&Maryland,	Grand,	T. Baker,	4.00	
McNab&Illin's,	National,	J. N. Walker, M.		
Wash.&Illinois,	Occidental,	Worden & Pettit,	3.00	AM
95 N. Meridian,	Pyle,	W. H. Porter,	1.50	8
Ills.&Louisiana,	Spencer,	Gray, Aikman&Co.,		
Jeffersonville,	Morgan's,	S. P. Morgan,		
Kendallville,	**Kelly's,**	J. B. & J. D. Kelly,	2.50	AL L
Knightstown,	Shipman's,	David Shipman,		
Kokomo,	Hauser's,	W. A. W. Hauser,		
Lafayette,	Lahrs',	Thos. Baker & Co.,	3.00	ANN
La Grange,	Cornell's,	Cornell Bros.,		
La Porte,	Merrill,	C. H. Hilton & Co.,	2.00	AI I
"	Tea Garden,	V. W. Axtell,	2.00	AI H
Lawrenceburg,	Anderson's,	B.T&W.S.Anders'n	1.25	AC B 7
Lebanon,	Rose's,	J. H. Rose,		
Liberty,	Commercial,	I. T. Ham,	1.75	AF C
Logansport,	Murdock,	Jones&Richardson,	3.00	14
Loogotee,	Burton's,	E. Burton,		
Madison,	Continental,	C. Hablizel,	2.00	AG 10
"	Western,	Henry Niesse,	2.00	AI 8 15
Marion,	McVickers,	Wm. McVicker,		
Martinsville,	Branham's,	Daniel Branham,	1.50	5
Metz,	Metz,	C. Rakestraw,		
Michigan City,	Jewell,	H. R. Harris,	2.00	
Mishawka,	Wilcox,	H. N. Wilcox,		
Mitchell,	Albert,	I. B. Faulkner,	2.00	AI G
Mt. Vernon,	Stewart's,	Mrs. A. Stewart,		
Muncie,	Haines',	S. T. & C. Haines,		
New Albany,	Central,	Thos. J. Fullenlove,	2.50	AJ I
New Castle,	Junction,	Wm. Clawson,	2.00	7
Noblesville,	Wainwright's,	Col. Wainwright,	2.00	AI I 18
North Vernon,	Snodgrass',	T. J. Snodgrass,	2.00	AI 7 13
Orland,	Burnham's,	Morris Burnham,		
Osgood,	Ellis',	J. V. W. Ellis,		
Peru,	Keller's,	John S. Keller,		

INDIANA.

TOWN.	HOTEL.	PROPRIETOR.			
Pleasant Lake,	Bigler's,	Wm. Bigler,	2.00	AH	G ..
Plymouth,	Empire,	Flemming & Son,			
Reynolds,	Junction,	James Evans,			
Richmond,	Tremont,	John Elliott,			
Rochester,	Wallace's,	R. Wallace,			
Rockport,	Eigenmann's,	Philip Eigenmann,			
Rushville,	Wilson's,	J. S. & O. S. Wilson,			
Seymour,	Schafer's,	Caspar Schafer,			
Shelbyville,	Morrison's,	Mrs. S. J. Morrison,	1.00	AA	A ..
Shoals,	Heckman,	John S. Lamb,	2.00	AH	9 ..
South Bend,	National,	L. H. Packard,	2.00	AG	G ..
"	St. Joseph,	John G. Greenwalt,	2.00	AG	G 18
Spencer,	National,	Evans & Son,	2.00	AI	5 ..
Terra Haute,	National,	Heinly&M'Coskey,	2.00		
Thorntown,	Adair's,	J. S. Adair,			
Tipton,	City,	Mrs. A. French,			
Union City,	Branham's,	S. Branham,			
Valparaiso,	Gould's,	Austin R. Gould,			
Vernon,	Storey's,	T. J. Storey,			
Vincennes,	La Plante,	John D. Cox & Co.,	2.50	AI	J 22
Wabash,	Tremont,	Mrs.M.A.Newman,			
Warsaw,	Kirtley,	G. W. Greene,	2.00		
Washington,	Harris',	Wm. Harris,			
Westville,	Coles',	Zina Cole,			
Winchester,	Ross',	Jack Ross,			
Worthington,	Osborn's,	K. B. Osborn,			

ILLINOIS.

TOWN.	HOTEL.	PROPRIETOR.				
Albion,	Bowman's,	Wm. Bowman,	2.00	AH	C	..
Aledo,	Button,	E. Carter,	2.00	AI	D	..
Altamount,	Rissler,	Joel B. Risster,	...	...	..	..
Alton,	Moore's,	L. W. Moore,	...	...	..	..
Altona,	Hopkins',	S. B. Hopkins,	...	...	..	..
Amboy,	Passenger,	Fred Hepburn,	2.00	AH	..	..
Annawam,	Dart's,	A. Dart,	...	...	..	..
Arcola,	Sullivan's,	Frank Sullivan,	...	...	..	..
Ashton,	Welton's,	W. B. Welton,	...	...	..	..
Astoria,	American,	John Sinig,	2.00	...	..	..
Assumption,	Commercial,	Frank T. Rasbach,	2.00	AG	G	15
Aurora,	Empire,*	Benj. Bisbey,	2.00	AI	D	..
Barrington,	Jayne's,	Wm. M. Jayne,	...	...	..	..
Barry,	Barry,	Mrs. L. De Haven,	1.25	AF	5	9
Batavia,	Smith's,	C. E. Smith,	...	...	..	..
Beardstown,	Virginia,	Tice Misenheimer,	1.25	....	5	..
Belleville,	Hinckley,	N. Hall,	2.00	AF	D	..
Belvidere,	**Truesdall's**	W. H Truesdall	2.00	AG	G	14
"	Julien,	Tousley&Sheridan,	2.00	AH	G	15
Bement,	Royal's,	Thomas Royal,	...	...	..	..
Bloomington,	Ashley,	Sill & Crammer,	3.00	....	..	..
"	St. Nicholas,	S. J. Stickney,	2.00	AF	F	..
Brighton,	Cottage,	Mrs. KateB.Glenny	2.00	AI	G	..
"	Moore's,	W. C. Moore,	1.50	AF	E	..
Brimfield,	Brimfield,	D. Belcher,	1.75	....	7	..
Buda,	Buda,	Albert Rhodes	2.00	AG	G	..
Buckley,	Afton,	S. A. Andrews,	2.00	AH	D	..
Bunker Hill,	Johnston's,	Benj. Johnston,	...	...	..	..
Bushnell,	National,	E. C. Hess,	1.50	AF	6	10
Cairo,	St. Charles,	Jewett,Wilcox&Co.	3.00	AL	L	..
Cambridge,	Whipple's,	S. E. Whipple,	...	...	..	..
Canton,	Churchill,	Samuel T. Burrell,	2.50	AL	14	..
"	**City,**	A. A. Hemenover,	2.00	....	7	..
Carrollton,	St. James,	Philip Fay,	...	...	..	..
Centralia,	Centralia,	Oscar Hughes,	2.50	....	9	..
Champaign,	Champaign,	P. Coffey,	1.25	....	5	..
"	Philipp's,	Wm. Nash,	2.00	AJ	J	..
Charleston,	Charleston,	J. W. B. Grove,	2.00	....	6	..
Chebanse,	Van's,	Vanorman & Maxwell,	...	...	..	..
Chenoa,	Matteson,	S. Houchin,	1.50	AE	E	15

ILLINOIS.

TOWN.	HOTEL.	PROPRIETOR.	
Chicago.			
LaSalle & Van-Buren-sts.,	Atlantic,	Wm. L. Newman & Co.	2.50 AI J ..
R'ndolph&Can'l	Barnes',	J. F. Latshaw,	1.00 EG ....
143 Madison,	Brevoort,	H. M. Thompson,	....
140 Madison,	Burke's,	Michael Burke,	1.50 EK ....
Wabash-ave. & Monroe,	Clifton,	Wilton A. Jenkins,	....
De'rborn&Lake	Commercial,	H. G. Pulling,	2.50 AL 14 ..
Clinton&Madi'n	Gault,	J. H. Cummings,	2.50 ....
Mich-av&Ja'k'n	Gardner,	C. H. Gaubert,	....
29 N. Wells,	Hatch,	John T. Corcoran,	2.00 .... 8 ..
220 E. Wash'g'n,	Irving,	E. C. Davenport,	.75 E ....
145 Dearborn,	Kuhn's,	Kuhn & Thorp,	.75 EE ....
Central-ave. & S. Water,	Massasoit,	Albert W. Longley,	....
State & Wash'n,	Metropolitan,	Swift & Rowland,	2.50 AL L ..
150 Wabash-ave.	Nevada,	Thomas Kendrick,	....
Clark&Rand'h,	**Sherman**,	Bissell & Hulbert,	3.00 AP 18 ..
22d & Wabash-av.	Woodruff,	J.W.Boardman&Co	3.50 ....
118 5th-ave.,	Wood's,	Enoch Wood,	2.00 .... 12 ..
Chilicothe,	Will's,	James Will,	2.00 AH 7 ..
Clay City,	Mound,	Emanuel Coontz,	2.00 AF 5 ..
Clayton,	Clayton,	James A. McCoy,	1.00 AF 4 ..
Columbia,	Angerer's,	John Angerer,	....
Cortland,	Cortland.	B. B. Parkhurst,	1,50 AG E 12
Coultersville,	New York,	Mrs. E. F. Philipps,	2.00 AI I 18
Danville,	St. James,	Watson Bros.,	2.00 .... 11 ..
Decatur,	National,	John McEvoy,	1.50 AE D 9
"	St. Nicholas,	N. Lauxe & Bro.,	....
De Soto,	De Soto,	J. V. Brown,	2.00 AH A ..
Dixon,	Cheney's,	P. Cheney, Jr.,	....
Dundee,	Bowman's,	John Bowman,	....
Dunleith,	Sutler's,	C. J. Sutler,	....
Du Quoin,	Story's,	Story & Pugh,	....
Dwight,	**Clifton**,	James Furman,	2.00 AE E ..
East St. Louis,	East St. Louis,	Julius Philipps,	2.00 AH 7 ..
Edwardsville,	St. James,	H. Kirkpatrick,	2.00 AI I ..
Effingham,	Fleming's,	Mrs.M.B.Fleming,	....
Elgin,	Waverly,	S. Lasher & Son,	2.00 ....
Elmwood,	Oldfield,	Silas Oldfield,	....
Evanstown,	Mattison's,	S. A. Mattison,	....
Ferris,	Ferris,	John B. Orr,	1.50 AH E 15
Flora,	Major's,	H.R. & S.J.Major,	....

TOWN.	HOTEL.	PROPRIETOR.		
Freeport,	Brewster,	J. S. Gates,		
Fulton,	Robinson's,	B. Robinson,		
Galena,	De Soto,	William Blewett,	2.00	
Galesburg,	American,	James Poling,	2.00	6
"	Brown,	R. H. Mead,	3.00 AK	K
"	National,	Cram Brothers,	2.00 AF	E
Geneseo,	Miller's,	Abraham Miller,		
Gilman,	Onderdonk's,	Henry Onderdonk,		
Grand Tower,	Tremont,	Frank Baronowsky	2.00 AF	F 17
Greenfield,	Sherman,	Brown & Moore,		
Greenville,	Victor,	J. Williams & Son,	2.00 AI	I
Harvard,	Ayer's,	E. G. Ayer,	2.00 AI	7
"	Harvard,	F. S. Nearing,	1.50	5
Havana,	Sanford's,	Geo. H. Sanford,		
Highland Park,	Central,	Harvey R. Greene,	2.00	12
"	Eagle,	Albert Orthoff,	2.00 AI	D
"	HighlandPark,	L. D. Mansfield,	2.50 AN	10
Jacksonville,	Dunlap's,	W.F.Dunlap & Co.	3.00 AM	M
Joliet,	National,	M. L. Adams,	2.00	10
"	St. Nicholas	S. A. Jenks,		
Kankakee,	Exchange,	Louis Carignon,		
Keithsburg,	Central,	C. C. Woodin,	2.00 AF	F 14
Kinmundy,	Squier's,	Wm. C. Squier,	2.00 AI	I
La Harpe,	Union,	Aquilla Claycomb,		
Lanark,	Lanark,	Samuel Dietrick,		
La Salle,	Harrison,	F. Harrison,	2.00	11
Leland,	Barnes',	Thos. Barnes,		
Lincoln,	Spilty's,	Martin Spilty,		
Macomb,	Randolph,	A. V. Brooking,	2.00 AI	I 18
Manteno,	Blessing's,	Isaac Blessing,		
Marseilles,	Pilling's,	J. Pilling,		
Marshall,	Sherman,	Henry Briscoe,	2.00 AI	I
Matteson,	Matteson,	L. D. Mills,	2.00 AH	7
Mattoon,	Essex,	Daniel Messer,	3.00 AL	11
Mendota,	Passenger,	C. F. Taylor,	3.00	
Moline,	Reese's,	Chas. Reese,		
Monmouth,	Baldwin's,	H. Baldwin,	2.00 AI	
Morris,	Clifton,	John B. Kage,	1.50 AE	E
"	Goodrich,	H. T. Garfield,	2.00 AF	F
Morrison,	Bailey's,	B. C. Bailey,		
Mound City,	Kelly's,	P. M. Kelly,		
Murphysboro,	Logan,	Dr. Jas. L.Skinner,	2.00 AI	G 14

ILLINOIS. 95

TOWN.	HOTEL.	PROPRIETOR.	
Naperville,	Stutenoth's,	Stutenoth & Son,	...
Neponset,	Neponset,	N. Conner,	2.00 A H H 16
New Athens,	Fries',	George Fries,	...
Olney,	Garst's,	J. B. Garst & Co.,	...
Orion,	Western,	John O. Valentine,	2.00 AI I ..
Ottawa,	White's,	M. White,	2.00 AI I 16
Pana,	St. James,	Col. E. N. Owen,	2.00 AI I 18
Paris,	Paris,	J. F. Anthon & Son	2.00 .... 7 ..
Paxton,	Warner's,	Jacob Warner,	...
Pekin,	Tazewell,	W. A. Tinney,	...
Peoria,	City,	H. S. De Vies,	2.00 AE G ..
"	Central	E. Philipps,	...
"	Peoria,	Chas. H. Deane,	2.50 AL .. ..
"	Merchants	Clark & Son,	...
Perry Springs,	Perry Springs,	B. A. Watson,	2.50 AI I ..
Petersburg,	Wilcox,	L. Wilcox,	...
Pinckneyville,	Sullivan's,	J. M. Sullivan,	...
Princeton,	American,	Sackett&Bushnell	2.00 AJ I ..
Quincy,	Occidental,	T. Rogers,	2.00 AI J ..
"	Quincy,	Miller & Morris,	...
"	Tremont,	Louis Miller,	3.00 AM .. ..
Raleigh,	Raleigh,	T. S. Mitchell,	...
Rantoul,	Martin's,	H. & B. Martin,	...
Richview,	American,	S. T. Howard,	...
Rockford,	Holland,	H. N. Starr,	2.00 AI 11 ..
"	American,	Mrs. J. R. Williamson	2.00 .... 6 ..
Rock Island,	Bellows',	J. M. Bellows,	...
"	Harper's,	Ben. Harper,	...
"	New Rock Island,	A. M. Guild,	2.00 x ....
"	Union,	John Mueller,	...
Sandwich,	Transient,	David Bloom,	2.00 AI I ..
"	Sandwich,	Joseph Dyas,	2.00 ....
Seneca,	National,	Henry Betterman,	...
Shawneetown,	Jones',	Jones & Norton,	...
Shelbyville,	National,	J. M. McKibben,	2.00 AF F ..
Somonauk,	Godell's,	J. M. Godell,	...
Springfield,	City,	W. D. Chenery & Sons,	...
"	Leland's,	H. S. Leland & Co.,	3.00 ....
"	Revere,	Joel Johnson,	2.00 AH H 18
"	St. Nicholas,	John McCreery,	2.00 AI J ..

ILLINOIS

TOWN.	HOTEL.	PROPRIETOR.		
Sterling,	Wallace,	J. Youngs & Son,	2.00	.... 10 ..
Sullivan,	Eden's,	Joseph E. Eden,		....
Taylorsville,	Long's,	Thomas Long,		....
Tuscola,	Beach's,	E. Beach,	2.00	....
Urbana,	Thurman's,	D. F. Thurman,	2.00 AI	7 ..
Vandalia,	Vandalia,	Geo. W. Turner,	2.00 AI	I ..
Vermont,	National,	J. P. McCaughey,	1.50 AF	.... ..
"	Vermont,	J. B. Laws,	1.50 AF	5 ..
Warren,	Burnett,	Solon Way,	2.00	.... 7 ..
Warsaw,	Warsaw,	E. G. Simms.	2.00 AE	D ..
Waukegan,	Sherman,	F. Converse,	1.50	.... 7 ..
"	Waukegan,	C. A. Murray,	2.00	.... 10 ..
Waverly,	Church's,	Levi Church,		....
White Hall,	Amos',	Mrs. M. T. Amos,		....
Woodstock,	Sherwood's,	Geo. N. Sherwood,		....

MICHIGAN.

TOWN.	HOTEL.	PROPRIETOR.		
Adrian,	Central	J. J. Allen & Co.,	2.00	.... 12 ..
"	Lawrence's	Marion Lawrence,	2.00 AJ	H ..
Albion,	Goodrich's	L. S. Goodrich,		....
Allegan,	McDuffy's	H. D. McDuffy,		....
Ann Arbor,	Gregory's	A. A. Gregory,		....
Attica,	Nichols'	A. D. Nichols,		....
Augusta,	McCord's	John L. McCord,		....
Bangor,	Watson's	Jeremiah E. Watson		....
Battle Creek,	American	James Williams,		....
"	Bristol	A. L. Larkin	1.60 AE	F 18
"	Potter's	Henry Potter,	2.50 x	.... ..
Bay City,	Campbell	C. A. Jay,		....
"	Ontario	John Conroy,	1.00 AA	A 9
Benton Harbor,	Nichols'	E. Nichols,		....
Berlin,	Cottage	M. V. Fisk,	1.00	.... 4 ..
Bridgeport,	Clark's	N. J. Clark,	2.00 AI	7 10
Brighton,	Union	Robt. Brigham,	1.50 AF	5 9
Buchanan,	Tremont	Mrs. S. Dann,		....
Burr Oak,	Frazier's	Wm. Frazier,		....
Cedar Springs,	Otis'	Otis & Smith,		....
Charlotte,	Sherwood's	G. W. Sherwood,	2.00	.... 10 ..
Chesaning,	Gleason's	J. T. Gleason,		....
Clam Lake,	Mitchell	Bodwell Bros.,		....
Clare,	Stage	J. B. Slattery	2.00	.... 6 ..

MICHIGAN. 97

TOWN.	HOTEL.	PROPRIETOR.		
Climax,	Wilson's	J. O. Wilson,		
Cold Water,	Bridge	Don. P. Cushman,	1.50 AE	E 14
Constantine,	Root's	H. E. Root,		
Coopersville,	Earle's	Eli P. Earl,		
Corunna,	Waverly	L. J. Clark,		
Dearborn,	Johnson's	Benj. Johnson,		
Decatur,	Duncomb	Delos B. Carroll,		
Detroit.				
Michigan & Wash'gton Av.	Antisdell's	W. W. Antisdell,	2.00	14 ..
Griswold & Congress St.	Howard	Hamilton & Clark,	2.00	12 ..
Jefferson Av. & Shelby,	Michigan Ex.	Lyon & Porter,	2.50	
Grand River & Cass Ave.,	Perkins'	Wm. Perkins, Jr.,	1.25 AC	D ..
Jefferson Av. & Randolph,	Revere	O. W. Penney,	2.00 x	.. --
Randolph & Atwater,	St. Lawrence	G. Wohlfarth,	1.50 AF	6 ..
Dowagiac,	Spring	E. Harmon,	2.00	5 ..
Dundee,	Potter's	J. M. Potter,		
E. Saginaw,	Bancroft	J. B. Norcross,	2.50	
"	Everitt	C. L. Snell,	2.50 AK	10 ..
Eaton Rapids,	Frost	PorterW.Knowles,		
Escanaba,	Tilden	Jas.W.Hutchinson,		
Fenton,	Everitt	King & Algoe,		
Flint,	City	Jas. McDonnell,		
"	Northern	H. C. Clement,		
"	Sherman	Wm. H.Fay & Co.		
Flowerville,	Flowerville	Button & Sweet,		
Frankfort,	Delbridge	Jas. McKelvey,		
FremontCentre,	Dehass'	Mrs. A. DeHass,		
Fruitport,	Pomona	W. T. Ball & Co.,		
Galesburg,	Mrs. Galligan's	Sarah J. Galligan,	2.00 AI	5 ..
Grand Haven,	Kirby	Edward Killian,	2.00	10 ..
Grand Ledge,	Dennison's	F. T. Dennison,	2.00 AI	.. ..
"	Exchange	P. V. Campbell,	1.00 AB	A ..
Grand Rapids,	Bennett's	Wm. H. Bennett,	1.25 AC	C ..
"	Eagle	J. R. Johnson,		
"	Rathburn	A. R. Antisdell,	2.00 AI	I ..
"	Sweets	Lyon & Pickering,		
Grass Lake,	Kingsley's	Wm. Kingsley,		
Greenville,	Hutchins'	S. G. Hutchins,		

4

TOWN.	HOTEL.	PROPRIETOR.	
Hanover,	Courtney's	Geo. Courtney,	....
Hartford,	Jackson	James Bassette,	....
Hillsdale,	Smiths	O. H. Green,	2.00 .... 14 ..
Holland,	City	E. Kellogg & Son,	....
Holly,	Andrews'	John E. Andrews,	....
Houghton,	Douglass	Thos. Cullyford,	....
Hudson,	Comstock's	C. M. Comstock,	....
Imlay,	Bancroft	Charles Palmer,	2.00 AH G ..
"	National	McEntee & Son,	1.50 AE E 10
Ionia,	Sherman	Henry Starkey,	....
Jackson,	Hibbards	J. M. Bradlee,	2.50 AL L ..
"	Hurd's	Smith & Hurd,	2.00 ....
Kalamazoo,	Burdick	W. H. Riley,	2.50 ....
"	Eureka	T. B. Smith,	1.00 AA A ..
Lansing,	Chapman	L. H. Bailey,	2.00 AF 7 ..
"	Lansing	Martin Hudson,	2.50 AL ....
Lapeer,	Abram's	James Abram,	....
Marquette,	Marquette	Jacob Kremers,	1.50 AC 7 ..
"	National	Thomas Casey,	2.00 AH 7 ..
Marshall,	Exchange	D. H. Way,	1.25 .... 5 ..
"	Witt's	W. H. Witt,	2.00 ....
Mason,	Moody's	F. P. Moody,	....
Midland,	Midland	Findlater & Alexander,	....
Monroe,	Strong's	Strong & Sons,	....
Muskegon,	American	John W. Coyer,	2.00 AG 7 ..
"	Washington	John H. Simons,	1.50 AE D ..
Negaunee,	Sporley's	Gottlieb Sporley,	....
New Baltimore,	Parker's	J. S. Parker,	....
Niles,	Bond	A. McKay,	2.00 AI D ..
"	Pike's	H. H. Pike,	2.50 AK L 25
Olivet,	Nelson's	L. C. Nelson,	1.50 AE E ..
Ontonagon,	Biglow	W. H. Beardsley,	....
Owosso,	**National**	A. J. Patterson,	2.00 ....
Paw Paw,	Dickeman	Chas. A. Sherman,	2.00 AI I 15
Pontiac,	Hodges'	Mrs. M. A. Hodges,	2.00 AI J ..
"	Astor	Mrs. Emeline Carter,	1.50 AE E ..
Pottersville,	Potter's	Geo. N. Potter,	....
Rockford,	Stinson's	H. N. Stinson,	1.50 ....
Saginaw City,	Taylor	Hopkins & Bither,	3.00 AM N ..
Schoolcraft,	Troxel's	Edmund Troxel,	....
Spring Lake,	Sinclair's	W. G. Sinclair,	1.50 AH D ..
Sturgis,	Exchange	E. W. Elliott & Son,	2.00 .... 9 ..

MICHIGAN.

TOWN.	HOTEL.	PROPRIETOR.			
St. Clair,	City	A. J. Cummings,	2.00	....	7 ..
St. Johns,	Perrin	John Sweeney,			
St. Joseph,	Plumley's	Daniel Plumley,			
Tecumseh,	Imerson's	Geo. H. Imerson,	1.50	AE	D ..
Three Rivers,	Three Rivers	Leonard Fisher,	2.00	AI	7 ..
Traverse City,	Gunton's	John S. Gunton,	2.00	....	11
Vicksburg,	McElvain's	J. W. McElvain,	2.00	AI I	16
"	Western	Levi Moffatt & Son,	1.00	AB	7 ..
White Pigeon,	France's	Geo. L. France.			
Wyandotte,	Biddle	C. J. Northrup,			
Ypsilanti,	Barton	Henry Landon,	1.00	AA	A ..

WISCONSIN.

TOWN.	HOTEL.	PROPRIETOR.			
Amherst,	Een's	Charles Een,			
Appleton,	Waverly	Turner&Morgan,			
Arcadia,	Burt's	Burt Brothers,	1.25	AC	C 10
Augusta,	Blair's	Hiram Blair,			
Baraboo,	Peck's	E. T. Peck,	1.00	AA	A 10
"	Western	Wm. B. Pearl,	2.00	AI	I 16
Bayfield,	Smith's	Philip W. Smith,	2.50	AI	I ..
Beaver Dam,	City	E. A. Parker,			
Beloit,	American	L. F. Wood,	1.50	AC	C 12
"	Goodwin	W. Saulsbury,			
Berlin,	Marshall's	Geo. Marshall,			
Branden,	Clark	Lawrence Bros.,	2.00	....	11 ..
"	Walker	Warren Hall,	1.50	AE	E ..
Burlington,	Western Union	John Steinhoff,	1.00	....	4 ..
Burnett,	Burnett	J. W. Childs,	2.00	AH	D ..
Chippewa Fall,	Waterman's	Waterman & Sons,	2.00	AF	F ..
Columbus,	Cooper's	H. C. Cooper,	2.00	AI	I 16
Darien,	Clark's	S. K. Clark,			
Darlington,	Lamar's	C. H. Lamar,			
Dartford,	Greenway's	D. Greenway,			
Delevan,	Andrus'	E. Andrus,			
De Pere,	White's	George E. White,			
Devils Lake,	Cliff	P.B.Parsons & Co.,	3.00	AM	18 ..
Dodgeville,	Hocking's	Joseph Hocking,			
Durand,	Carley	Joseph Barton,	1.00	AD	A ..
Eau Claire,	**Peabody**	Peabody & Robinson,	2.00	AG	G ..
Elkhorn,	Snyder's	J. H. Synder,			

WISCONSIN.

TOWN.	HOTEL.	PROPRIETOR.				
Evansville,	Spencer	A. L. Beebe'	2.00	AI	D	..
Fond Du Lac,	American	H. Shattuck,	....	....	..	..
"	Central	Wm. Korrer,	1.50	AD	D	11
"	Lewis	S. Oberrich,	1.50	AC	..	..
Fort Atkinson,	Davis'	J. H. Davis,	....	....	..	..
Fort Howard,	Broadway	C. McGinnis,	1.00	AE	..	..
Fox Lake,	American	F. A. Wallace,	2.00	AF	6	..
Geneva Lake,	St. Denis,	B. K. Cowles,	....	....	..	..
Grafton,	Dreyer's	John Dreyer,	....	....	..	..
Grand Rapids,	Roche's	William Roche,	2.00	AH	F	18
Green Bay,	Adams	George Smith,	1.00	....	5	..
"	Beaumont	Cozzens & Son,	....	....	..	..
"	First National	H. H. Hunt,	2.00	AI	I	..
Green Lake,	Oakwood S. R.	D. Greenway,	2.50	....	12	..
Hartford,	Wisconsin	John P. Gaetz,	1.50	AE	A	..
Horicon,	American	S. Streeter,	1.00	AD	A	..
Hudson,	St. Nicholas	Mrs. Lizzie Kelley	2.00	....	10	..
Janesville,	Spence's	J. Spence,	....	....	..	..
"	Williams	H. Tyrrell,	2.00	....	5	..
Jefferson,	Sawyer's	M. Sawyer,	....	....	..	..
Kenosha,	American	G. Aroltz,	2.00	....	7	..
"	**Water Cure**	E. Pennoyer,	2.00	....	7	..
Kilbourn City,	Finch's	Wm. H. Finch,	2.00	AI	I	..
La Crosse,	International	I. Reynolds,	....	....	..	..
Lancaster,	Lancaster,	L. Lisherness,	1.00	AA	A	..
Madison,	Capitol	W. H. Spaulding & Son,	....	....	..	..
"	Park	Mark H. Irish,	3.00	AN	..	..
"	Vibas	P.B.Parsons & Co.	3.00	AM	18	..
Manitowoc,	Franklin Hall,	Wm. Nallan,	1.00	AA	A	..
Marinette,	Le Roy's	J. Le Roy,	....	....	..	..
Menasha,	Vanghn	Philo Hine,	1.25	AC	C	..
Menomonee,	Hanson's	Hanson Bros.,	....	....	..	..
Milton Junct'n,	Foster	C. J. Foster & Co.,	....	....	..	..
Milwaukee.						
Ferry & S.Water St.,	Axter's	Axter&Picketson,	....	....	..	..
Ferry & S. Water,	Cream City	Chas. J. Dewey,	2.00	....	10	..
....	**Kirby**	Kirby & Chase,	2.00	AJ	J	21
....	**Newhall**	John F. Antisdall,	3.50	AN	N	..
313 Fourth St.,	Union	Wm. Hock,	1.00	....	5	..
Mineral Point,	Walker's	Wm. Walker,	....	....	..	..
MinnesotaJunc.	Young's	Thomas Young,	....	....	..	..

WISCONSIN.

TOWN.	HOTEL.	PROPRIETOR.			
Montello,	American	P. Gorman,	1.50 AC	C	..
Muscoda,	Smalley's	John Smalley,	....	...	...
Neenah,	Pfeiffer's	A. Pfciffer,	....	...	..
Neilsville,	Rossman's	Jacob Rossman,	....	...	..
Oconto,	Beyer	J. S. Dolan,	2.00	....	10 ..
Oconomowoc,	Townsend's	CopelandTownsend...	....	...	..
Omro,	Larrabee's	F. D. Larrabee,	....	...	...
Oshkosh,	Beckwith	Beckwith&Fargo,	....	...	...
"	Revere	Moore & Cameron	....	...	.. ..
"	Seymour	Joseph Stringham,	....	...	...
Ozaukee,	Dallas'	John Dallas & Son,	....	...	...
Platteville,	Stevens'	J. R. Stevens,	....	...	...
Plymouth,	Central	Wm. Siseher,	1.25	....	4 ..
Portage City,	City	Richard Gage,	1.50 AD		.. ..
"	Ellsworth	Alex. McDonald,	2.00 AH	7	..
Prairie DuChien,	Dousman	J. F. Williams,	....	...	...
Princeton,	Schneider's	J. P. Schneider,	....	...	..
Racine,	**Congress Hall**	Seneca Raymond,	3.00 AL	L	28
"	Huggins	C. H. Jarrell,	2.00 AI	J	..
Randolph,	Clement's	E. Clement,	1.50 AE	A	..
Ripon,	Mapes	John Weisgerber	2.00 AI	I	..
Rubicon,	Rubicon	Marcus Trumer	1.25	....	4 ..
Schleisingerville,	Menger's	George F. Menger	....	...	...
Sheboygan,	Beekman	Halsted & Stearns	2.00 AI	1	..
"	Pape's	Fred. Pape,	2.00 AH	8	..
Sparta,	Warner	J. D. Condit,	2.50 AJ	J	..
Superior,	Avery's	M. L. Avery,	....	...	..
Tomah,	Merkley's	M. H. Merkley,	....	...	...
Watertown,	American	A. B. Hitchcock,	....	...	..
"	**Rail Road**	Nelson W. Pierce,	2.00 AI	I	..
Waukesha,	Schaffer's	M. Schaffer,	....	...	...
Waupun,	Western	H. Hopkins,	1.50	....	5 ..
Wausau,	**Forest**	C. A. Single,	2.00	....	7 ..
"	Paradis'	L. Paradis,	2.00 AH	10	..
Whitewater,	American	Luther Cadman,	1.00 AA	....	..
"	Exchange	G. P. Dustin,	2.00	...	.. ..
Winneconne,	Union	James Gingles,	1.00	....	4 ..

MISSOURI.

TOWN.	HOTEL.	PROPRIETOR.		
Albany,	Albany	W. G. Williams,	1.75 AC	C 12
Alexandria,	Warner's	E. Warner,		
Allenville,	Allenville	P. N. O'Brien,		
Arrow Rock,	Arrow Rock	....	1.50 AE	F ..
Booneville,	Central	I. M. Seconejost,	1.50	5 ..
"	McPherson's	Mrs.M.J.McPherson	2.50 AK	L ..
Brookfield,	Blossom's	G. N. Blossom,		
Buffalo,	Hovey's	E. Hovey,		
Brunswick,	Brunswick	John Knechler,	2.00 AI	7 ..
Callao,	Owens'	T. F. Owens,		
Cameron,	Combs'	Chester D. Combs	2.00 AI	8 ..
Canton,	Downs'	Wm. Downs,		
Cape Girardeau,	St. Charles	Z. Block,	2.00 A	11 ..
Chilicothe,	Browning	S. G. Swetland,	2.00	7 ..
Clinton,	Allen's	Robert Allen,		
Columbia,	McKim's	Robert J. McKim,		
Danville,	Arnold's	Wm. H. Arnold,		
De Witt,	Planters	P. P. Guillett,	2.00 AI	D ..
Fredericktown,	Kent's	Peter Kent,		
Fulton,	Whaley's	David L. Whaley,		
Gallattin,	Eagle	M. P. Cloudas,		
Glascow,	City	Franz Michels,	1.50 AH	5 ..
Glenwood,	Broadway	W. F. Staples,		
Hamilton,	Goodman's	Wm. Goodman,		
Hannibal,	Continental	W. H. Grubb,	2.00	7 ..
"	National	Geo. A. Kettering,	2.00 AI	....
Hermann,	Niehoff's	Bernard Niehoff,		
Holden,	Bell's	Richard Bell,	2.00	9 ..
Huntsville,	Austin	Mrs. M. McCampbell,		
Independence,	Merchants	M. S. Morgan,	2.00 AI	I ..
Ironton,	Ironton	D. S. Drake,	2.00 AJ	I ..
Jefferson City,	A. & P. Dining Hall	J. W. Mabrey,	2.00 AI	....
"	Central	J. A. Huegel,	1.50 x	....
"	Madison	B.H.McCarty & Son,	3.00 x	....
"	Nichols'	Samuel Nichols,	2.00 AI	7 ..
"	Pacific	J. W. Mabrey,	2.00 AI	G ..
Jonesburg,	Camp's	Josiah Camp,		
Kansas City,	Commercial	Emanuel Fielder,	1.50 AF	D ..
"	La Clede	John H. Burke,		
"	Lindell	Charles Richards,	3.00 AM	I ..
Kahoka,	Tremont	A. Kearns,	1.00 AB	A ..

MISSOURI.

TOWN.	HOTEL.	PROPRIETOR.			
Keytesville,	Mackay's	Andrew Mackay,			
Kirksville,	American	J. S. Pool,			
La Grange,	Tremont	S. H. Williams,	2.00		
Lamonte,	Lamonte	W. S. Files,	1.50	AF	F ..
Lathrop,	Daniels'	John O. Daniels,			
Lebanon,	La Clede	Altaway & Co.,	2.00	AI	.. ..
Lexington,	Johnson's	Baylis & Johnson,	2.50	....	10 ..
Liberty,	Courtney's	A. C. Courtney,			
Louisiana,	City	Mrs. J. Bracey,	2.00	....	7 ..
"	Sladeck's	Mrs. A. Sladeck,			
Macon,	Scott's	J. V. Scott,			
Marshall,	Ming's	W. O. Ming & Son,			
Maryville,	Central	E. A. Hagan,	2.00	....	7 ..
"	Shady Glen	J. S. Bramble,	2.50	AI	J ..
Mexico,	Brown's	J. W. Brown,			
Miami,	Miami	Wm. Mayfield,	2.00	AE	A ..
Missouri City,	City	Mrs. L. E. Dickinson,			
Moberly,	Merchants	Brown & Bro.	2.00	AH	7 ..
"	**Virginia**	Mrs. Mary L. Swan,	2.00	....	9 ..
Monroe,	Livingston's	Mrs. S. Livingston			
Montgomery,	Hutchison's	D. C. Hutchison,	1.00	....	5 ..
Palmyra,	National	Geo. W. Lane,	2.00	AI	I ..
Plattsburg,	Commercial	J. S. Baker,	2.00	AI	7 ..
Pleasant Hill,	Shermans	F. D. Mers,	1.50	....	7 ..
Richmond,	Hudgens'	Wm. B· Hudgens,			
Rolla,	Shaw's	H. M. Shaw,			
Sedalia,	New Lindell	John Y. Carpenter	2.00	AG	E ..
Shelbina,	American	M. B. Mullaney,	1.50	....	7 ..
"	Waverly	Arthur Connely,	2.00	AI	7 ..
St. Charles,	Faut's	J. S. Faut,	1.75	AH	E 12
"	Galt	S. W. Logan,	2.00	AI	I 16
St. Joseph,	International	T. K. McGuire,	2.00	AI	D ..
"	Occidental	Fred. Hall,	2.00	AI	I ..
"	Pacific	Gilkey & Abell,	3.00	AL	.. ..
"	Planters	Joseph James,	4.00	AQ	P ..

St. Louis.

826 N. 4th St.,	American	Geo. Ikemeyer,	1.25	AF	6 ..
2d & Walnut,	Barnum's	L. A. Pratt,	3.00	..:..	.. ..
7th cor. Poplar,	Clarendon	Thomas Randle,	2.00	AJ	I ..
101 S. 10th,	Gaffney's	James Gaffney,	1.00	....	5 ..
Broadway & Washington,	German	E. A. Amsbaugh,	50	EC	.. ..

MISSOURI.

St. Louis.	HOTEL.	PROPRIETOR.		
Biddle&B'way	Girard	V. Adami & Bro.,	1.50	A D ....
5th&Chestnut,	La Clede	J. W. Malin & Son,	4.00	....
Wash. & 6th,	McDowell's	W. C. McDowell,	1.50	.... 7 ..
B'way & N. Market,	Mound City	Lewis Babbitt,	1.50	A F E ..
Main & N. Market,	N. Missouri R. R.	Martin N. Willman,	1.00	.... 5 ..
2d & Olive,	Olive St.	W. K. Peterman,	2.00	A J J ..
5th & Walnut,	St. James	R. Boyle,	3.00	.... 18 ..
817 N. 4th,	St. Nicholas	Enos Jennings,	2.50	A x ....
Carr & B'way,	Western	John M. Gilman,	1.50	.... 9 ..
Tipton,	St. Louis	D. B. Tolle,	2.00	.... 5 ..
Trenton,	Powell's	Joseph Powell,		....
Union,	Johnson's	C. Johnson,		....
Warrenton,	Warrenton	Bockhorst & Bro.		....
Warrensburg,	Ead's	Mrs, J. D. Eads,	2.00	A I I ..
"	Simmons'	E. K. Simmons,	2.00	A I I ..
Warsaw,	Rice's	L. O. Rice,		....
Washington,	Remmert's	Wm. Remmert,		....
Weston,	Weston	John Throckmorton		....

IOWA.

TOWN.	HOTEL.	PROPRIETOR.		
Ackley,	Bolander's	R. Bolander,		....
Afton,	Oriental	Tryon & Powers,		....
Agency City,	Hardin's	John Hardin,		....
Albia,	Cramer's	G. P. Cramer,		....
Alden,	Davis'	M. J. Davis,		....
Ames,	West's	Wm. West,		....
Anamosa,	Anamosa	Fowler & Clothier,		....
Atlantic	Pacific	S. W. W. Straight,	2.00	A E D 14
Avoca.	Jones'	John Jones & Son,		....
Bellevue,	Bower's	Henry Bower,		....
Belle Plain,	Sherman	John F. Dunn,	2.00	A 9 ..
Bentons Post,	Des Moines	B. M. Patten,	2.00	A G G 15
Boone,	Phipps'	C. E. Phipps,		....
Brighton,	Fleak's	L. B. Fleak,		....
Brooklyn,	American	John Jordan,	1.00	A B B ..
Brush Creek,	Shambaugh's	Mrs. B. A. Shambaugh,		....

IOWA.

TOWN.	HOTEL.	PROPRIETOR.	
Burlington,	Barrett	Stephen Long,	3.00 AM N ..
"	Central	Geo. Bomgardner,	2.00 .... 7 ..
"	Lawrence's	W. B. Lawrence,	3.00 AL M ..
"	Union	Christ Geyer,	2.00 ....
Cedar Falls,	Burr's	Burr & Davis,	... .
Cedar Rapids,	Browns	Eno & Philipps,	... .
"	Park Avenue	Adams & Williams	2.00 AH 7 ..
Centreville,	McKee's	Alex. McKee,	... .
Charles City,	Union	A. G. Bearup,	2.00 ....
Charlton,	Bates'	B. F. Bates,	... .
Cherokee,	Farmers Exchange	Ely Spencer,	2.00 .... 7 ..
Clarinda,	Clarinda	John Beam,	2.00 .... 10 ..
Clarence,	Post's	E. E. Post,	2.00 AF E 10
Clarksville,	Peet's	Geo. K. Peet,	... .
Clinton,	Revere	Moulton & Conine,	2.50 ....
Council Bluffs,	Biggs'	W. L. Biggs,	1.50 AF C ..
"	Metropolitan	L. D. Hurrin,	2.00 AI .. ..
Davenport.			
4th & Perry St.	Burtis'	J. J. Burtis,	... .
....	Farmers	Herman Stepfen,	1.00 .... 5 ..
Main & 2d St.,	Newcombs	Dan'l Gould,	2.50 AL L ..
3d & Iowa,	Pennsylvania	James Robbins,	1.00 .... 4 ..
Front & Harrison,	Scotts	J. J. Humphrey,	2.00 .... 10 ..
404 W. Second,	St. Louis	D. Brammer,	... .
Decorah,	Winnesheik	J. E. Dowe,	2.00 AI J 21
Denison,	Commercial	E. J. Trowbridge,	2.00 AI F ..
Des Moines,	Avenue	Joseph Wellsby,	1.50 AB A ..
De Witt,	Gates'	J. M. Gates,	... .
Dexter,	Young's	J. J. Young,	... .
Dubuque,	Julian	W. W. Woodworth	3.00 AM .. ..
"	Key City	W. W. Pine,	... .
"	Lorimer	Barnard Bros.	2.50 AJ K ..
"	New Jefferson	N. G. Theisen,	1.00 .... 5 ..
"	Tremont	John W. Parker,	2.00 AE D ..
"	Weston	V. Stoltz,	1.00 AA 4 ..
Dyersville,	Wheeler's	George Wheeler,	... .
Eddyville,	Amos'	Mrs. L. F. Amos,	2.00 AJ 7 ..
Eldora,	Commercial	M. L. Edginton,	2.00 AI F ..
Fairfield,	Johnson's	Nathan Johnson,	2.00 .... 7 ..
Farley,	American	Stephen Goodale,	2.00 .... 7 ..
Farmington,	Brock's	F. Brock,	2.00 AI D ..

IOWA.

TOWN.	HOTEL.	PROPRIETOR.		
Fort Dodge,	Occidental	J. H. Waters,	2.00	.... 10 ..
Fort Madison,	Metropolitan	George Anthes,		... ...
Glidden,	Glidden	N. D. Thurman,	2.00 AI	I ..
Grand Junct'n,	**Ashley**	J. P. Gulick,	2.00	.... 5 ..
Grinnell,	Grinnell	Johnson & Christian	2.00 AI	I ..
Hamburg,	Carson's	J. J. Carson,		... ...
Hampton,	Hampton	John Coloney	2.00 AI	7 ..
Independence,	Merchants	C. A. Backus,	2.00 AI	.... ..
Indianola,	Watson's	J. C. Watson,		... ...
Iowa City,	Pinney's	Charles Pinney,	2.00 AH	H 18
Iowa Falls,	Jones'	L. P. Jones,	2.00 AI	I ..
Janesville,	Newell's	M. Newell,		... ...
Jefferson,	Dick's	J. Dick,		... ...
Keokuk,	Barrett's	W. Barrett,		... ...
"	Hardin's	E. Hardin,	2.00 AI	J ..
"	Patterson's	W.A. & J. C. Patterson		... ...
Lansing,	St. Nicholas	John Schinzel,		... ...
Le Mars,	Le Mars	L. K. Bowman,	2.00	... ...
Lyon,	Sherwood's	Philo Sherwood,		... ...
Malcolm,	Central	Jas. Duffers & Son,	2.00 AI	6 ..
Manchester,	Manchester	Robert Johnson,		... ...
Marengo,	Clifton	J. S. Shaw,		... ...
Marion,	Park Place	George W. Wilson,	2.00 AF	D ..
Marshalltown,	**Boardman**	A. I Lindsay,	3.00	.... 18 ..
Mason City,	Commercial	G. L. Bunce,	1.50	.... 5 ..
McGregor,	Bigelow's	L. Bigelow,		... ...
Mechanicsville,	City	T. H. Williams,		... ...
Monona,	Monona	H. M. Handy,	1.25 AC	C ..
Monticello,	Burnett	Charles Ryan,	2.00	.... 10 ..
Mt. Pleasant,	Whiting's	Samuel S. Whiting,		... ...
Muscatine,	National	J. D. DeMoss,	2.00	.... 11 ..
"	Commercial	R. M. Baker,	2.50 AJ	14 ..
Newton,	Richmond's	Townsend Richmond,	2.00	.... 7 ..
Nora Springs,	Brown's	Spencer & Brown,		... ...
Osceola,	Ball's	John M. Ball,		... ...
Oskaloosa,	St. James	Joe C. Allen,	2.00 AI	G ..
Ossian,	National	H. B. George,	2.00 AI	I ..
Ottumwa,	Ballingall	David Hodge,		... ...
Pella,	Ohio	B. Gardner,		... ...
Shellsburg,	Lewis'	Andrew Lewis,		... ...
Shelby,	Shelby	Lucius Benham.	2.00 AH	G ..

IOWA.

TOWN.	HOTEL.	PROPRIETOR.		
Sioux City,	Clifton	John Weber,	2.00 A I	E ..
"	St. Elmo	G. W. Lower,	2.00	10 ..
"	Wilson's	John Wilson,	2.00 A I	G ..
Springville,	Bruce's	H. Bruce,	... ...	.. ..
State Centre,	St. James	J. E. McLafferty,	2.00 A I	I ..
Tipton,	Fleming's	Catharine Fleming,	... ...	.. ..
Victor,	National	F. P. Hutchins,	2.00 A G	G ..
Vinton,	Cole's	S. W. Cole,	... ...	.. ..
Wapello,	Iowa	Geo. Van Horn, Sen.	1.50 A E	E ..
"	Wapello	Wm. Rabold,	2.00	G ..
Washington,	Palmer's	Palmer & Dowing,	... ...	.. ..
Waterloo,	Central	J. H. Williams,	2.00	10 ..
"	Cedar Valley	John Mesick,	1.00 A B	.. ..
Waverly,	Keeney's	C. C. Keeney,	... ...	.. ..
Webster City,	Hamilton	I. W. Dyer,	2.00	7 ..
West Side,	Hartney's	A. Hartney,	2.00 ...	.. ..
Wilton,	McIntyre's	R. A. McIntyre,	... ...	.. ..
Winterset,	Clapp's	D. P. Clapp,	... ...	.. ..
Woodbine,	Pugsley's	G. W. Pugsley,	... ...	.. ..

MINNESOTA.

TOWN.	HOTEL.	PROPRIETOR.			
Anoka,	Kimball,	Matt Laib,	2.00	AI	I 18
Austin,	Grand Central,	J. S. Corning,	2.00	AI	7 ..
"	Fleck's,	Fleck & Hay,	2.00	AI	I ..
Belle Plain,	Castells,	J. Castell & Co.,	...	...	...
Brainerd,	Leland's,	W. H. Leland,	...	...	...
Brownsville,	Roster's,	M. S. Roster,	...	...	...
Caledonia,	Caledonia,	Williams&Stafford,	...	...	...
Chatfield,	Durham's,	W. H. Durham,	...	...	...
Duluth,	Decker's,	N. Decker,	...	...	...
Elk River,	Colson's,	S. Colson,	...	...	...
Faribault,	Barron's,	H. E. Barron,	2.00	AI	J 20
"	National,	John Misgeu,	1.25	AD	5 ..
Hastings,	Reed's,	William E. Hull,	2.00	AI	I ..
Jackson,	Ashley's,	Welch Ashley,	...	...	...
Lake City,	Brown's,	T. Brown,	...	...	...
Le Roy,	Hall's,	J. B. Hall,	...	...	...
Mankato,	Mankato,	G. C. Burt,	2.00	...	11 ..
Minneapolis,	First National,	Bigelow&Clark,	2.00	AI	I 18
"	Nicolet,	M'Kibbin&Vosburg	3.00	AMN	..
Minneiska,	Minneiska,	P. Carroll,	2.00	...	...
New Ulm,	Brust's,	Chas. Brust,	...	...	...
Northfield,	Bingham's,	J. T. Bingham,	...	...	...
Owatoma,	Arnold's,	Arnold & Hastings,	...	...	...
Red Wing,	National,	F. S. Field	2.00	AI	I ..
Reed's L'd'g,	Pauly's,	James Pauly,	...	...	...
Rochester,	Merchants',	W. W. Reed,	1.50	AF	F ..
Shakopee,	National,	James Heth, Jr.,	2.00	AI	9 ..
"	Occidental,	G. W. Gellenbeck,	2.00	AH	D ..
Stillwater,	Sawyer,	Albert Lowell,	2.00	AI	E ..
St. Charles,	Hall's,	Henry Hall,	...	...	...
St. Cloud,	Haywood's,	J. E. Haywood,	...	...	...
St. Paul,	American,	N. Pottgieser,	2.00	AH	F ..
"	Cosmopolitan,	D. Upman,	2.00	AI	I 16
"	European,	R. E. Hicketheir,	2.00	...	10 ..
"	Merchants',	A. Allen,	3.00	...	18 ..
"	Minnesota,	H. Aureden,	1.00	AA	A ..
"	Park Place,	E. V. Holcombe,	...	...	...
"	Sherman,	Ferris & Kissner,	2.50	AI	G ..
St. Peter,	Viltz,	Mrs. Nicholas Viltz,	...	...	...
Wabasha,	Reck's,	Felix Reck,	...	...	...
Waseca,	Mulvany's,	John Mulvany,	...	...	...
Wells,	Wells,	John P. Burke,	2.00	AI	7 ..
WhiteBearLake,	Leip's,	Wm. Leip,	...	...	...
WinnebagoCity,	Collins',	E. G. Collins,	...	...	...
Winona,	Cockrell's,	F. E. Cockrell,	...	...	...

TOWN.	HOTEL.	PROPRIETOR.			
Atchinson,	Atlantic,	W. E. Clute,	2.00	AI	E ..
Baxter Springs,	Planters',	Thomas Jones,	2.00	....	6 ..
Blue Rapids,	Reed's,	McPherson & Reed,			
Burlington,	Stafford,	D. C. Stafford,			
Burlingame,	Richardson's,	M. W. Richardson,			
Chanute,	Wickard's,	Wickard Bros.,			
Chetopa,	National,	Kellman & Pratt,			
Council Grove,	Commercial,	Hamilton & Sager,			
Effingham,	Benton's,	M. R. Benton & Co.,			
Ellsworth,	Grand Central,	A. Larkin,	2.50	....	10 ..
Emporia,	Luther's,	Wm. B. Luther,			
Eudora,	Copp's,	Henry Copp,	1.00	AA	A ..
Fort Scott,	Noonan's,	C. D. Noonan,			
Frankfort,	Weston's,	E. Weston,			
Garnett,	St. James,	Smith I. Gordon,	2.00		
Girard,	Andrus,	A. A. Hulett,	2.00	AJ	J ..
Hiawatha,	Smouse's,	Sam'l Smouse,			
Humbolt,	Tremont,	Charles Apitz,			
Independence,	Warner's,	Warner & Bro.,			
Iola,	Leland,	B. D. Allen,	2.00	....	5 ..
Junction City,	Kelly's,	Mrs. J. Kelley,			
Lawrence,	Durfee,	J. C. Walten,	2.00	....	11 ..
"	Eldridge,	H. H. Luddington,	3.00	AMM	..
Leavenworth,	Mansion,	Leonard & Madden,	2.00	....	8 ..
Marysville,	Sherman,	G. D. Swearingen,	2.00	AI	I ..
Newton,	Rasure's,	D. Rasure,			
Olathe,	American,	Cochran & Burch,	2.00	AI	H ..
Osage City,	Osage City,	Reece & Robbins,	3.00	....	8 ..
Paola,	Union,	M. Donovan,			
Parsons,	Lockwood's,	W. G. Lockwood,			
Pleasanton,	Pleasanton,	Josiah Sykes,	2.00	....	5 ..
Salina,	City,	Taylor&McQuary,	3.00		
Seneca,	Seneca,	J. E. Smith,	2.00		
Thayer,	Baldwin,	C. T. Ewing,			
Topeka,	Fifth Avenue,	J. B. Fluno,			
"	Gordon's,	J. C. Gordon,	2.00	AH G	15
"	Teft,	McMeekin & Hindman,	3.00	AM	L ..
Troy,	City,	John G. Light,	1.50	AF	F 15
Wamego,	Ames',	John W. Ames,	2.00	AI	I ..
Waterville,	Waterville,	Sam'l M. Shaw & S'n,	1.00	AA	A ..
Wathena,	Carson's,	C. C. Carson,	1.00	AB	.. ..
"	City,	Mrs. Ernst. Muecke,	1.00	AB	B ..
Wichita,	Lamb's,	Fraser & Lamb,			
Wyandotte,	Hollaford's,	H. A. Hollaford,			

NEBRASKA.

TOWN.	HOTEL.	PROPRIETOR.		
Ashland,	Snell's,	J. H. Snell,		
Beatrice,	Emory,	Mrs.A.G.Spellman,	2.50 AI	J 19
Columbus,	Clother's,	G. & C. D. Clother,		
Crete,	Howard's,	Mrs. C. J. Howard,		
Dakotah City,	Ogden's,	John G. Ogden,		
Falls City,	Union,	J. G. Good,	2.00 AG H	
Fremont,	Joss',	Jacob Joss,		
Humboldt,	Norton's,	J. T. Norton,		
Lincoln,	Snyder's,	Snyder & Smith,		
Nebraska City,	Johnson's,	M. T. Johnson,		
Omaha,	American,	Henry Lauer,	1.25 AA A	9
"	California,	J. B. Vandaniker,	1.50 AE D	..
"	City,	E. T. Page,		
"	Omaha,	Mrs. L. Walter,		
Plattsmouth,	Saunders,	J. H. Liggett,	2.00 AI I	..

NEVADA.

TOWN.	HOTEL.	PROPRIETOR.	
BattleMount'in,	BattleMount'inR.	V. Kelly,	2.00 AHH ..
Carson City,	Tufly's,	George Tufly,	
Eureka,	Gillen's,	William Gillen,	
Oreana,	Exchange.	Eben P. Torry,	2.00 AH G ..
Reno,	Barnes',	A. H. Barnes,	
"	Harris,	J. D. Pollard,	2.25 .... 12 ..
Virginia City,	Ryan's,	W. B. Ryan,	
Wells,	Mitchell's,	J. F. Mitchell,	

DAKOTA.

TOWN.	HOTEL.	PROPRIETOR.	
Elk Point,	Bovee's,	A. Bovee,	
Yanktown,	St. Charles,	Cresner & Co.,	
"	Smith's,	H. H. Smith,	

IDAHO.

TOWN.	HOTEL.	PROPRIETOR.	
Boise City,	Greene's,	J. H. T. Greene,	
Silver City,	Eastmans',	H. Eastman,	

WYOMING.

TOWN.	HOTEL.	PROPRIETOR.		
Cheyenne,	Jones',	G. M. Jones,	....	
"	Inter-Ocean,	B. L. Ford,	4.00 A R R	..
Evanston,	Donald's,	Booth&McDonald,	....	
Laramie City,	Worth's,	N. C. Worth,	....	
Rawlins,	Railroad,	Capt. James Lang,	3.00 AN	....

COLORADO.

TOWN.	HOTEL.	PROPRIETOR.			
Central City,	National,	R. B. Smock,	2.50	 10	..
"	Teller,	W. H. Bush,	4.00 AQ R	..	
Canon City,	Sheetz,	M. M. Sheetz & Co.	....		
Denver,	Ford's,	B. L. Ford,	....		
"	Tremont,	J. C. Veatch,	3.00 AI	I 17	
Greeley,	Boynton's,	N. M. Boynton,	....		
Idaho Springs,	Beebe's,	Fayette W. Beebe,	....		
Pueblo,	Burgess',	John T. Burgess,	....		
Trinidad,	Trinidad,	Winram & Leavitt,	....		

UTAH.

TOWN.	HOTEL.	PROPRIETOR.		
Salt Lake City,	Valley	Dahl&Sorenson,	2.00 A H H	..
"	Walker	R. G. Lansing,	4.00 A 21	..

CALIFORNIA.

TOWN.	HOTEL.	PROPRIETOR.		
Auburn,	Auburn,	John J. Smith,	2.00 12	..
Bakersfield,	Escalet's,	Ernest Escalet,	....	
Benicia,	Wienman's,	J. Wienman,	....	
Brighton,	Magnolia,	Perkins & Orr,	....	
Chico,	Chico,	Ira A. Wetherbee,	2.50 AL 12	..
Davisville,	Marden's,	W. H. Marden,	....	
Dixon,	City,	Frahm Bros.,	1.50 AD B	..
Dutch Flat,	Dutch Flat,	J. B. Marcovitch,	....	
Ellis,	Ludwig's,	S. Ludwig,	....	
Eureka,	Manning's,	Patrick Manning,	....	
Galt,	Harvey's,	C. W. Harvey,	....	
Gilroy,	Hanna,	Shaw & Robinson,	....	

TOWN.	HOTEL.	PROPRIETOR.		
Grass Valley,	Benson's,	Wm. H. Benson,		
Haywards,	Halfway House	J. P. Halm,		
Healdsburg,	Skagg's,	A. & E. Skagg,		
Los Angelos,	Lafayette,	Fluhr & Gerson,	2.50	15 ..
"	United States,	Hammel & Denker,	1.50	9 ..
Marysville,	Van Deveer's,	Mrs. E. E. V'ndeveer		
Napa,	American,	T. F. Raney,		
Nevada,	Gentry's,	R. B. Gentry,		
Oakdale,	Grand Central,	Harry Weaver,		
Oakland,	Tubb's,	Jno. M. Lawler & Co.	3.00 AP	
Petaluma,	American,	W. B. Matzenbach,	3.00 AK	12 ..
Placerville,	Varozza's,	Varozza & Co.,		
Quincy,	Plumas,	J. E. Edwards,		
Red Bluff,	Pott's,	J. D. Potts,		
Redwood City,	Ayers',	Charles Ayres,		
Sacramento,	Arcade,	T. Guinean,	3.00	18 ..
"	Brooklyn,	J. E. Mooney,		
"	Western,	Wm. Land,		

San Francisco,

319 Sansom-st.,	American Exchange,	W. & T. Bryan,	2.50	14 ..
210 Bush,	Brooklyn,	Kelly & Andrews,	2.50	14 ..
824 Kearney,	International,	H. C. Partridge,	2.00	12 ..
Mont'g & Sutler,	Lick's,	James Lick,	3.00	21 ..
531 Sacramento,	Overland,	John E. Slinkey,	1.50	
933 Kearney,	Prescott,	Otto F. Becker,	1.50 AE	E ..
214 Broadway,	Western,	John Higgins,	1.00	5 ..
San Jose,	Auzwall,	S. W. Churchill,		
"	Atlantic,	John Johnson,	1.00 AA	6 ..
"	N.Y. Exchange,	Barker & Towne,	2.00	10 ..
San Leandro,	Union,	George Giblin,		
Santa Barbara,	Morris',	James F. Morris,		
Santa Clara,	Cameron's,	John H. Cameron,		
Santa Cruz,	Pacific Ocean,	J. H. Hoadley,	3.00 AL	
Santa Rosa,	Keissing,	J. A. Hudnall,	1.50 AH	F ..
Sonora,	Bemis',	Oliver L. Bemis,		
Stockton,	Rossi's,	Antonio Rossi,		
"	Stockton,	Schneider & Holman		
Tehama,	Heider's,	Christian Heider,		
Truckee,	Truckee,	John F. Moody,	2.50 AN	

CALIFORNIA.

TOWN.	HOTEL.	PROPRIETOR.	
Vallejo,	Brownlie's,	John Brownlie,	....
"	Golden Eagle,	John Heninger,	....
Watsonville,	Billing's,	A. W. Billings,	....
Woodland,	Capital,	A. S. House,	....
Yosemite Valley,	Black's,	Alexander G. Black,	....
Yreka,	Rohrer's,	John B. Roher & Co.,	....

OREGON.

TOWN.	HOTEL.	PROPRIETOR.	
Portland,	Cosmopolitan,	Zieber & Holten,	....
"	Clarendon,	Hallett & Kimball,	....
"	Occidental,	Andrus & Smith,	1.50 AH 9 ..
"	Quimby's,	L. P. W. Quimby,	....
"	Stark's,	L. Stark,	....
Salem,	Chemeketta,	Thomas Smith,	2.00 A x ....

CANADA.

ONTARIO.

TOWN.	HOTEL.	PROPRIETOR.			
Acton,	Agnew's	Robert Agnew,	2.00 x	.. ..	
Almonte,	Davis'	Sam'l H. Davis,	1.50 x	.. ..	
Amherstburg,	Brown's	Ellis Brown,	....		
"	Temperance	Alexander Wilson,	1.00 AA	4	8
Argyle	McKay's	John McKay,	2.00 x	.. ..	
Arnprior,	Devine's	H. & B. Devine,	2.00 x	.. ..	
Arthur,	Green's	C. C. Green,	1.50 x	.. ..	
Aurora,	Wait's	James Wait,	1.50 x	.. ..	
Aylmer,	Parker's	Sidney Parker,	2.00 x	.. ..	
Barre,	Arnall's	A. Arnall,	2.00 x	.. ..	
Beamsville,	Rodgers'	Bernard Rodgers,	1.50 x	.. ..	
Beaverton,	Hamilton's	Alex'r Hamilton	2.00 x	.. ..	
Belle Evart,	Hanmer's	E. V. Hanmer,	1.00 AA	4	8
Belleville,	Doyle's	John Doyle,	2.00 x	.. ..	
"	Kyle's	S. Kyle,	2.50 x	.. ..	
Berlin,	Dopp's	George Dopp,	2.00 x	.. ..	
Bothwell,	Campbell's	Dan'l Campbell	....		
"	Royal	James Dickson,	1.00 AA B	12	
Bowmansville,	Brodie's	Thos. Brodie, Jr.,	2.00 x	.. ..	
"	Shaw's	Thos. Shaw,	1.50 x	.. ..	
Bradford	Algeo's	Robert Algeo,	2.00 x	.. ..	
Brampton,	Murphy's	John Murphy,	2.00 x	.. ..	
"	Revere	W. Beck,	1.00 AA	4	..
Brantford,	Batson's	Hugh Batson,	3.00 x	.. ..	
"	Hatch's	Philander B. Hatch	2.00 x	.. ..	
"	Palmer's	John C. Palmer,	2.50 x	.. ..	
Brockville,	Howe's	Howe & Marston,	....		
"	St. Lawrence	McCarney & Barnes	1.50 AF F	16	
Bronte,	Bronte	J. M. Trillor,	.75 ED	.. ..	
Brussells,	Parker's	John Parker,	1.50 x	.. ..	
Caledonia,	Hinds'	Fred. Hinds,	2.00 x	.. ..	
"	Trotter's	James Trotter,	2.00 x	.. ..	
Cannington,	Lapp's	Samuel Lapp,	2.00 x	.. ..	
Cayuga,	Humphrey's	T. Humphrey, Jr.,	2.00 x	.. ..	
Chatham,	Garner's	John Garner,	2.00 x	.. ..	
"	Green's	John Green,	1.50 x	.. ..	
"	Rutley	Frederick Soop,	1.00 AB	.. ..	

ONTARIO. 115

TOWN.	HOTEL.	PROPRIETOR.				
Clifford,	Dopfers	John Dopfer,	2.00 x	.. ..		
Clifton,	Ellis'	John Ellis,	2.00 x	.. ..		
"	Rosli's	G. Rosli,	2.00 x	.. ..		
Cornwall,	American	A. J. Maley,	2.00	AE	F	16
Drayton,	Markle&Shaws'	Markle & Shaw,	2.00 x	.. ..		
Dundas,	Cain's	Patrick Cain,	2.00 x	.. ..		
"	Scace's	George F. Scace,	2.00 x	.. ..		
Dunville,	Nevin's	John H. Nevin,	2.50 x	.. ..		
Elora,	Biggar's	Thomas Biggar,	2.00 x	.. ..		
Galt,	Colwell's	Thomas Colwell,	1.50 x	.. ..		
"	Lavin's	Peter Lavin,	2.00 x	.. ..		
Guelph,	Ellis'	Thomas Ellis,	2.50 x	.. ..		
"	Jones'	William Jones,	2.00 x	.. ..		
Hamilton.						
59 W. King St,	American	F. W. Bearman,	1.00	....	7	..
Market Sq. & McNab,	Anglo American	E. R. Carpenter,	2.00 x	.. ..		
York & Park,	Commercial	S. H. Wheeler,	1.00	AD	5	..
204 Bay,	Metropolitan	C. Hutton,	2.00 x	.. ..		
James&Merrick	Royal	Hood & Bro.,	2.50	AJ	J	..
Ingersoll,	Adair's	John Adair,	2.00 x	.. ..		
"	Daley	S. H. Wheeler,	1.00	AA	A	..
Kingston,	Anglo American	E. Milsap & Co.,	2.50	AH	G	18
"	British "	Swales & Davis,	2.00 x	.. ..		
London,	Lloyd	Thomas Lloyd,	2.50 x	.. ..		
"	Queens	Lewis Jefferis,	2.50 x	.. ..		
Ottawa,	Albion	John Graham,	1.50 x	.. ..		
"	Daniels'	S. Daniels,	1.50 x	.. ..		
"	Hamilton's	R. Hamilton,	2.00 x	.. ..		
"	Russell	James A. Souin,	3.50	AK	14	..
"	Windsor	Samuel Daniels	2.00	AI	.. ..	
Peterboro,	Phelan's	Edward Phelan,	2.50 x	.. ..		
Port Hope,	Queens	George Mackie,	2.00	AF	F	16
"	Crawley's	Elias Crawley,	....	....		
Sarnia,	Bellchamber	Joseph Huggins,	2.00	AF	F	16
Stratford,	Albion	D. L. Caven,	2.00	....	10	..
St. Catharines,	Rees'	John F. Rees,	2.00 x	.. ..		
St. Thomas,	Cole's	John Cole,	2.00 x	.. ..		
"	Wilcox's	Jacob Wilcox,	2.00 x	.. ..		

TOWN.	HOTEL.	PROPRIETOR.			
Dorchester,	Wilbur's	Willard D. Wilbur,	2.00 x	....	
Frederickton,	Barker	Robinson & Colby	2.00 x	....	
"	Queen	J. P. Burnham,	1.50 AF	....	
Monckton,	King's	D. C. King,	2.00 x	....	
St. John.					
Prince Wm. St.	Barnes'	A. B. Barnes & Co.	2.00	....	
22 King Sq.,	Park	H. Fairweather,	2.00 AH	I ..	
21 King,	Revere	Adam C. A. Wells,	1.00 AB	A ..	
146 Prince Wm.	Royal	T. F. Raymond,	....		
King & Charlotte	United States	James Hinch,	....		
Duke & Germain	Victoria	George W. Sweet,	3.00 AN	20 ..	
St. Stephen,	Rudge's	W. Rudge,	1.50 x	....	
Sussex,	Fairweather's	G. M. Fairweather	1.50 x	....	
Woodstock,	Stephenson's	Matt. Stevenson,	2.00 x	....	

NOVA SCOTIA.

TOWN.	HOTEL.	PROPRIETOR.			
Amherst,	**Lamy's**	I. & I. R. Lamy,	1.50 AC	9 18	
Annapolis,	Salter's	William Salter,	2.00 x	....	
Bridgetown,	Miller's	Misses Miller,	1.50 x	....	
Bridgewater,	Commercial	B. W. C. Manning,	1.50 x	....	
Five Islands,	Tremont	Mrs. J. Broderick,	1.00 AB	B ..	
Halifax,	Acadian	George Nichols,	....		
"	American	Campbell & Bacon	1.00 AB	5 ..	
"	Carlton	B. W. Cochran,	....		
"	Halifax	H. Hesslein & Sons	2.50 AI	J ..	
"	**International**	Archibald Nelson,	1.50 AF	F ..	
"	South	Wm. T. Fanning,	....		
"	Waverly	Mrs. Romans,	....		
Liverpool,	International	G. S. Mack,	1.50 x	....	
Pictou,	Revere	Charles L. Rood,	1.50 AF	F ..	
Truro,	Grand Central	Alexander Carter,	1.25 AB	A ..	
Windsor,	Avon	E. A. McBride,	1.25 AC	A ..	
"	Gibson's	Thomas Gibson,	....		
Yarmouth,	American	James R. Scribner,	1.50 AF	F ..	
"	Yarmouth,	James H. Baxter,	2.00 AF	F 16	

ONTARIO.

TOWN.	HOTEL.	PROPRIETOR.			
Toronto.					
Front & Yonge,	American	George Brown,	2.00	AJ	J ..
256 W. Front,	Brittania	George Blackbird,	....	....	.. ..
Front & West,	Marlborough	M. A. Trotter,	....	....	.. ..
92 Front,	The Queens	McGaw & Winnett	3.50	AO	.. ..
41 W. King,	Revere	J. B. Riley & May,	2.00	x	.. ..
York & King,	Rossin	G. P. Shears,	3.00	AN	.. ..
York & Front,	Walker	David Walker,	2.00	AI	12 ..
Woodstock,	Emigh's	Hiram Emigh,	....	....	.. ..
"	Royal	P. Farrell,	1.50	....	5 ..
Windsor,	Barrett's	Edward Barrett,	2.50	x	.. ..
"	McLaughlin's	Peter McLaughlin,	2.00	x	.. ..

QUEBEC.

TOWN.	HOTEL.	PROPRIETOR.			
Athabaska,	Boisclair's	George Boisclair,	1.50	x	.. ..
Danville,	McMann's	John McMann,	2.00	x	.. ..
Montreal.					
17 St. Gabriel,	Canada	A. Beliveau,	2.00	AH	H ..
246 St. James,	Ottawa	Browne & Perley,	3.50	AK	L ..
105 St. Paul,	St. Edward	Julien Gadona,	....	....	.. ..
13 Latour,	Victoria	R. Decker,	....	....	.. ..
Quebec,	Albion	Wm. Kirwin	2.50	AJ	14 ..
"	Clarendon	Mrs. G. Boyce,	....	....	.. ..
"	St. Louis	Willis Russell,	3.50	AO	N ..

INSTRUCTIONS FOR USING THE KEY.

The Key on the opposite page is referred to by the figures, and capital letters following the names &c. of the Hotels as follows, for instance at the American Hotel in Boston, of which Messrs. Lewis Rice & Son are the Proprietors, the terms are $3.00 per day, no rates given for parts of a day, and no reduction; the same with the Sturtevant Hotel in New York, of which Lewis & George S. Leland, are the Proprietors, $4.00 per day.

R. S. Bailey & Son of the Franklin Square Hotel, Philadelphia, regular rates $3.00 per day; Commercial Travellers with my GUIDE rate as in upper column A J per day, or parts of day, and as in lower column A J per week or parts of week, or 75 cents for dinner or lodging, and 50 cents for Tea or Breakfast, and $2.00 per day, $6.00 for three days, $9.00 for five days, and $12.00 per week.

Maurice L. Harnett of Bresnans Hotel, Savannah, kept on both American and European plan, the A following the rate in all cases meaning that the Hotel is kept on the American plan and the E following that it is kept on the European plan, and as in the case of Bresnaus Hotel, that it is kept on both plans. On the American plan as in upper column A I per day and parts of day, and as in lower column A H per week, or parts of week, and as in bottom column E F on the European plan per day, per week, or parts of week.

The x following the rates means that while I am quite positive such are the rates per day, as I have received them from what I consider a very trustworthy source, is not to be relied upon, but where no x appears I have received the information direct per letter from the landlord, which letters are now on file in my office.

S. R. following the name of the Hotel, means that it is a summer resort, and the prices are higher usually in summer, than the rates given.

The letter M following the name of the Proprietor means that he is the Manager or Superintendent instead of Proprietor.

KEY TO ROE'S HOTEL GUIDE.

HOTELS KEPT ON THE AMERICAN PLAN.

	AA	AB	AC	AD	AE	AF	AG	AH	AI	AJ	AK	AL	AM	AN	AO	AP	AQ	AR
Dinner	.25	.40	.40	.40	.40	.50	.50	.50	.50	.75	.75	.75	.75	1.00	1.00	1.00	1.00	1.25
Tea	.25	.30	.30	.40	.40	.40	.40	.50	.50	.50	.50	.75	.75	.75	.75	1.00	1.00	1.00
Lodging	.25	.40	.40	.50	.40	.50	.50	.50	.50	.75	.75	.75	.75	1.00	1.00	1.00	1.00	1.25
Breakfast	.25	.30	.30	.40	.40	.40	.40	.50	.50	.50	.50	.75	.75	.75	.75	1.00	1.00	1.00
Dinner and Tea	.50	.60	.70	.70	.80	.80	.90	.90	1.00	1.00	1.25	1.50	1.50	1.50	1.75	2.00	2.00	2.25
Tea and Lodging	.50	.60	.70	.70	.80	.80	.90	.90	1.00	1.00	1.25	1.50	1.50	1.50	1.75	2.00	2.00	2.25
Lodging and Breakfast	.50	.60	.70	.70	.80	.80	.90	.90	1.00	1.00	1.25	1.50	1.50	1.50	1.75	2.00	2.00	2.25
Breakfast and Dinner	.50	.60	.70	.80	.80	.80	.90	.90	1.00	1.00	1.25	1.50	1.50	1.50	1.75	2.00	2.00	2.25
Tea, Lod'ng & Breakf'st	.75	.80	1.00	1.00	1.00	1.20	1.25	1.25	1.30	1.50	1.75	1.75	2.00	2.25	2.50	2.50	3.00	3.25
Lod'ng, Breakf'st&Din'r	.75	.80	1.00	1.00	1.00	1.20	1.25	1.25	1.40	1.50	1.75	2.00	2.00	2.25	2.50	2.75	3.00	3.25
Breakfast, Din'er & Tea	.75	.80	1.00	1.00	1.00	1.20	1.25	1.25	1.30	1.50	1.75	1.75	2.00	2.25	2.50	2.50	3.00	3.25
Dinner, Tea & Lodging	.75	.80	1.00	1.00	1.00	1.20	1.25	1.25	1.40	1.50	1.75	2.00	2.00	2.25	2.50	2.75	3.00	3.50
Board, per Day	1.00	1.00	1.25	1.25	1.50	1.50	1.50	1.75	1.75	2.00	2.00	2.50	2.50	3.00	3.00	3.50	4.00	4.00

BOARD.	AA	AB	AC	AD	AE	AF	AG	AH	AI	AJ	AK	AL	AM	AN	AO	AP	AQ	AR
One Day	1.00	1.25	1.25	1.50	1.50	1.50	1.75	1.75	2.00	2.00	2.50	2.50	3.00	3.00	3.50	3.50	4.00	4.00
Two Days	2.00	2.00	2.50	2.50	2.75	3.00	3.50	3.50	4.00	4.00	5.00	5.00	6.00	6.00	7.00	7.00	8.00	8.00
Three "	3.00	3.00	3.50	3.75	4.00	4.50	5.00	5.00	5.50	6.00	7.00	7.50	8.50	9.00	10.00	10.50	11.00	12.00
Four "	3.50	4.00	4.50	5.00	5.00	6.00	6.00	6.50	7.00	7.50	9.00	9.50	10.50	12.00	13.00	14.00	14.00	16.00
Five "	4.00	5.00	5.00	6.00	6.00	7.00	7.00	8.00	8.00	9.00	10.00	11.50	12.50	14.00	16.00	16.00	17.00	19.00
Six "	4.50	5.50	5.50	6.50	7.00	8.00	8.00	9.00	9.00	10.50	11.00	13.50	14.50	16.00	18.00	18.00	20.00	22.00
One Week	5.00	6.00	6.00	7.00	8.00	9.00	9.00	10.00	10.00	12.00	12.00	15.00	16.00	18.00	20.00	22.00	22.00	25.00

HOTELS KEPT ON THE EUROPEAN PLAN.

ROOM.	EA	EB	EC	ED	EE	EF	EG	EH	EI	EJ	EK
One Day	.25	.50	.50	.75	.75	1.00	1.00	1.25	1.25	1.50	1.50
Two Days	.50	.90	1.00	1.50	1.50	2.00	2.00	2.50	2.50	3.00	3.00
Three "	.75	1.30	1.50	2.00	2.25	3.00	3.00	3.75	3.75	4.50	4.50
Four "	1.00	1.70	2.00	2.50	3.00	3.75	4.00	4.75	5.00	5.75	6.00
Five "	1.25	2.00	2.50	3.00	3.75	4.50	5.00	5.75	6.25	7.00	7.50
Six "	1.40	2.25	2.75	3.50	4.50	5.25	6.00	6.75	7.50	8.25	9.00
One Week	1.50	2.50	3.00	4.00	5.00	6.00	7.00	7.50	8.50	9.00	10.00

LIBRARY OF CONGRESS

0 014 575 599 2

www.ingramcontent.com/pod-product-compliance
Lightning Source LLC
Chambersburg PA
CBHW020125170426
43199CB00009B/642